A 10-17555 (7-22-68)

I

THE STRUGGLE BETWEEN PRESIDENT JOHNSON AND CONGRESS OVER RECONSTRUCTION

STUDIES IN HISTORY, ECONOMICS AND PUBLIC LAW

EDITED BY

THE FACULTY OF POLITICAL SCIENCE OF COLUMBIA
UNIVERSITY IN THE CITY OF NEW YORK.

Volume VIII]   [Number 1

THE STRUGGLE

BETWEEN

PRESIDENT JOHNSON AND CONGRESS

OVER RECONSTRUCTION

BY

CHARLES ERNEST CHADSEY

AMS Press, Inc.

New York

1967

AMS Press, Inc.
New York, N.Y. 10003
1967

Manufactured in the United States of America

CONTENTS

PAGE

CHAPTER I. THEORIES PRIOR TO THE CLOSE OF THE WAR.

1. The Problem 7
2. Common Belief at Opening of Hostilities : The Crittenden Resolution 8
3. The Democratic Theory 10
4. Lincoln : The Development of his Theory 14
5. The Congressional Policy 18

CHAPTER II. JOHNSON'S THEORY : THE EXPERIMENT AND ITS RESULTS.

1. Conditions at Accession of Johnson 28
2. Lincoln vs. Johnson 28
3. Johnson's views before Accession 29
4. Speeches in the Spring after his Accession 30
5. Secret of his Attitude 32
6. Development of his Theory 34
7. Attitude towards Enfranchisement of the Negro . . . 41
8. Legislative Action in the South 42
9. The Defense of the South 46
10. Effect of the Attitude of the South upon the North . . 47

CHAPTER III. ATTITUDE OF CONGRESS TOWARDS THE EXPERIMENT : DEVELOPMENT OF THE CONGRESSIONAL THEORY.

1. Attitude of Parties towards the Administration at Beginning of the Session 49
2. Opening Scenes in Congress 50
3. The Annual Message : Debate on Reconstruction . . 55
4. The Freedmen's Bureau 59

5

PAGE

5. Johnson's Indiscreet Speeches in February, 1866 . . .   65
6. Civil Rights ; Other Bills   68
7. Report of Committee on Reconstruction   73
8. Authorized Measures of First Session   80

CHAPTER IV. THE CAMPAIGN OF 1866.

1. Crisis in the Cabinet   87
2. The New Orleans Riots   88
3. Administration Conventions   91
4. Anti-Administration Conventions   98
5. The Fall Elections   103
6. Action on the XIV Amendment   104

CHAPTER V. THE CONGRESSIONAL THEORY FULLY DEVELOPED.

1. The Second Session Convenes ; The Annual Message .   107
2. First Reconstruction Bill   109
3. First Supplementary Bill   117
4. Second Supplementary Bill   122
5. State Conventions   124
6. Third Supplementary Bill   125
7. Ratification of Constitutions   125
8. Acts Re-admitting States to Representation in Congress.   125

CHAPTER VI. THE IMPEACHMENT OF THE PRESIDENT.

1. Why Congress Wished to Impeach   127
2. What is an Impeachable Offense   128
3. The Opening Attack   129
4. The Work of the Judiciary Committee   131
5. The Attack Fails   132
6. The Limitation of Presidential Powers   133
7. The Tenure-of-Office Act   134
8. Struggle with Secretary Stanton   135
9. Articles of Impeachment   138
10. Attitude of Conservative Republicans   140
11. Conclusion   141

THE

STRUGGLE BETWEEN PRESIDENT JOHNSON AND CONGRESS

OVER RECONSTRUCTION.

CHAPTER I.

THEORIES OF RECONSTRUCTION PRIOR TO THE CLOSE
OF THE WAR.

1. THE war of the rebellion afforded opportunity for the people of the United States to obtain a far clearer conception of the powers and limitations of the federal constitution than had previously been possible, and settled beyond possibility of further debate some of the most important questions which had arisen since its interpretation as an "instrument of evidence" had begun. Yet when General Johnston had surrendered his army on April 26, 1865, virtually bringing the war to a close, the country found that one great constitutional question, a question of the highest practical importance, still remained unsolved; and for several years the best energies of our statesmen were occupied with its solution. Eleven of the States had for four years been in armed insurrection, but now, through superior force, they lay helpless at the feet of the Union. Under these circum-

stances, what was their constitutional relation to the federal government ?

Previous to the passage of the ordinance of secession by the convention of South Carolina in 1860, the nation never had been called upon to determine the status of a State which declared its relation to the federal government severed. Certainly if a State could establish its independence by war, the question, so far as such State was concerned, would have no significance; but as such a conclusion of the difficulty could not be considered for an instant, the status of the seceded State, both before and after the cessation of hostilities, immediately became an important subject of discussion. The gradual evolution of popular sentiment, from the belief that the dignity of a State should not be tampered with, to the belief that by an act of secession a State divested itself of all its rights and privileges as a State, and reverted to the condition of a Territory, forms an interesting chapter in the history of the unwritten constitution of the United States.

2. When the 37th Congress met on July 4, 1861, in pursuance of Lincoln's proclamation, the war had not been in progress long enough to show to the country the extreme gravity of the situation and the wideness of the gap which had arisen between the Southern States and the rest of the Union. The common belief was that unprincipled agitators, who represented only a small minority of the legal voters in the insurrectionary States, had obtained temporary control over the governments of these States, and were waging a war against the Union, in which they were unsupported by the majority; and that the latter would joyfully resume control of their governments as soon as the opportunity should be given them, which it was confidently believed would soon happen. That is, the war was to be carried on, not against the States which claimed to have seceded, but against a certain element of the Southern population.

The extreme solicitude felt by Congress for the proper preservation of the sovereign privileges of these States is shown by the practical unanimity with which a resolution submitted by Mr. Crittenden, on July 22, was carried, there being only two dissenting voices.[1] It declared the sense of the House to be that[2] " this war is not waged upon our part in any spirit of oppression, nor for any purpose of conquest or subjugation, nor purpose of overthrowing or interfering with the rights or established institutions of those States, but to defend and maintain the supremacy of the Constitution and to preserve the Union with all the dignity, equality, and rights of the several States unimpaired ; and that as soon as these objects are accomplished the war ought to cease." Three days later, Andrew Johnson, then a Senator from Tennessee, submitted the same resolution in the Senate,[3] where it was also carried with practical unanimity, although the discussion indicated a confused idea as to its exact significance.

But few months passed by before this staunch confidence in the rights of the States began to be shaken; a feeling of doubt had arisen which had not as yet resolved itself into a definite change of attitude, yet which was sufficient to prevent the re-endorsement of Mr. Crittenden's resolution, introduced by Mr. Holman, December 4, 1861, and tabled by a vote of 71 to 65.[4]

A series of resolutions introduced in the Senate by Mr. Davis of Kentucky, on February 13, 1862,[5] while preserving

[1] Scott, *Reconstruction during the Civil War*, 245 ff.

[2] *House Journal*, 1st Session, 37th Congress, pp. 123–5.

[3] Alexander H. Stephens, in *The War between the States*, uses this fact as a basis for the charge that Johnson was inconsistent in refusing to ratify the Sherman-Johnston Convention.

[4] *House Journal*, 2d Session, 37th Congress, p. 33.

[5] *Senate Journal*, 2d Session, 37th Congress, pp. 202–4.

in the main the principles then in vogue, assumed a some-what broader tone and expressed very clearly the belief of a large element of the thoughtful classes. Affirming the per-manency of the privileges of the people of the United States, it denied the criminality of the citizen who does not perform " his duties of loyalty and obedience, when the government fails to give him protection and security," and declared that the powers of the nation and State in the State are simply in suspension during a period of insurrection, and should be resumed, unimpaired, when the insurrection ceases. Here also was affirmed, in unmistakable terms, the inability of the States to secede, and the consequent obligation of the United States to preserve in these States republican forms of govern-ment. The guilty leaders should be punished, but the masses should receive amnesty; and immediately following the important admission was made that " if the people of any State cannot or will not reconstruct their state government, and return to loyalty and duty, Congress should provide a government for such State as a territory of the United States, securing to the people thereof their appropriate constitu-tional rights."

Here, in connection with the positive statement that a State cannot secede, and the implication that the insur-rectionary citizen may be upheld in his actions, was a clear expression of so-called extra-constitutional powers in treat-ing incorrigible States as territories. It would be interesting to know how these resolutions were viewed by the Senate, but they were laid on the table and never taken up for discussion.

3. During the opening days of the 3d Session of the 37th Congress, the question of the right to interfere with the States as States, was brought fairly before the House by a series of resolutions in which the policy of the extreme wing

of the Democratic party was expressed.[1] In them it is declared that "the Union *as it was*, must be restored and maintained, one and indivisible."[2] When this declaration is examined, with the President's preliminary proclamation of emancipation in mind, the significance of the three italicised words can be seen. The resolutions, after quoting the substance of the Crittenden resolution, further declared that "whoever shall pervert or attempt to pervert the same to a war of conquest or subjugation, or for the overthrowing or interfering with the rights or established institutions of any of the States, and to abolish slavery therein, or for the purpose of destroying or impairing the dignity, equality, or rights of any of the States, will be guilty of a flagrant breach of public faith and of a high crime against the Constitution and the Union." The same guilt was declared to attach to all who should "propose by federal authority, to extinguish any of the States of the Union, or to declare any of them extinguished, and to establish territorial governments within the same."

These resolutions, which were an open attack upon the presidential policy, were tabled by a vote of 79 to 50, a party vote. This fact is of significance as an evidence of the growing feeling in the House, that the sovereign rights of the States might be too highly considered, and that decided discipline of some kind might be found a measure of necessity. It began to be doubted whether in some of these States there could be found a sufficient number of loyal citizens to carry on the government without modifications of the old constitution and laws. At the same time the small majority by which the resolutions were tabled shows

---

[1] *House Journal*, 37th Congress, 3d Session, p. 43. Introduced December 5, 1862, by C. L. Vallandigham, whose subsequent career is well known. See Cox *Three Decades of Federal Legislation*, pp. 80–85.

[2] The italics are mine.

that the old idea still exercised a powerful influence in the House.

On December 14, 1863, resolutions were introduced by Mr. Finck,[1] and others two days later by Mr. Rollins,[2] which were very similar to the Crittenden resolution, and were introduced merely as expressions of the Democratic policy, since the Republican majority was too pronounced to permit their adoption.

From the beginning of the war, the policy of the Democratic party in the North was to bring about some agreement between the North and the South, by compromises and concessions, and should the issue finally be determined in favor of the Union even by dint of superior strength, to restore the Southern States to their former condition. In short, the theory held almost unanimously by Congress at the opening of the 37th Congress, was retained as the Democratic theory,[3] while the Republicans gradually modified their opinions, and with the progress of events developed a theory different from both the Democratic and the presidential theory.

Even after the proclamation of emancipation had come to be recognized as one of the natural results of the war, the policy of the Democratic party was unchanged except as necessarily modified by emancipation, and in the House, on February 8, 1864, Jacob B. Blair submitted resolutions[4] in which it was stated that " every State which has ever been, is still a State in the Union, and that when this rebellion shall have been put down, each of the so-called seceding States will have the same rights, privileges, and immunities under the Constitution as any one of the loyal States, except so far as the holding of African slaves in bondage is affected

---

[1] *House Journal*, 1st Session, 38th Congress, p. 48.   [2] *Ibid.*, pp. 65–6.

[3] See Cox, *Three Decades of Federal Legislation*, 123.

[4] *House Journal*, 1st Session, 38th Congress, pp. 238–9.

by the President's proclamation." These resolutions also repudiated " the doctrine advanced by some, that the so-called seceding States have ceased to be States of and in the Union, and have become territories thereof, or stand in the relation of foreign powers at war therewith."

But besides political declarations, the Democratic theory found other ways of expression in Congress. From the very commencement of the war, many of the leaders of the party were confident that hostilities could be brought to an end and peaceful relations restored by a convention of States, and several attempts were made to induce Congress to consider favorably some such plan.[1] As early as July 15, 1861, only eleven days after the convening of the extra session of Congress, Benjamin Wood introduced a resolution in the House,[2] which recommended that the governors of the several States " convene their legislatures for the purpose of calling an election to select two delegates from each Congressional district, to meet in general convention at Louisville, in Kentucky, on the first Monday in September next; the purpose of the said convention to be to devise measures for the restoration of peace to our country."

Again at the opening of the second session on December 4, 1861, joint resolutions were introduced by Mr. Saulsbury, in the Senate,[3] to appoint Millard Fillmore, Franklin Pierce, Roger B. Taney, Edward Everett, Geo. M. Dallas, Thomas Ewing, Horace Binney, Reverdy Johnson, John J. Crittenden, George E. Pugh, and R. W. Thompson, " commissioners on the part of Congress, to confer with a like number of commissioners to be appointed by the States " in rebellion,

---

[1] For a very able discussion of the " Efforts at Compromise, 1860–61," see Frederic Bancroft's article in *Political Science Quarterly*, vi, pp. 401–423.

[2] *Congressional Globe*, 1st Session, 37th Congress, p. 129.

[3] *Ibid.*, 2d Session, 37th Congress, part i, p. 8.

"for the preservation of the Union and the maintenance of the Constitution." The resolutions also provided that when the several States should have appointed their commissioners, hostilities should cease, "and not be renewed unless said commission shall be unable to agree," or "agreement shall be rejected either by Congress or by the aforesaid States."

One year later, December 2, 1862, a third attempt [1] was made by Mr. Davis, who submitted a joint resolution in the Senate (S. 104), proposing a convention from all the States to devise means for the reconstruction of the Union, and on May 30, 1864, Mr. Lazear submitted in the House, resolutions which were to authorize the President to "adopt or agree upon some plan upon which the decision of the great body of the people north and south may be secured upon the question of calling a convention composed of delegates from all the States, to which shall be referred the settlement of all questions now dividing the southern States from the rest of the Union, with a view to the restoration of the several States to the places they were intended to occupy in the Union."

During the later years of the war, after hope of success had begun to die out, some of the Southern States looked very favorably upon the plan; but nothing approximating such a convention resulted. [2]

4. At the beginning of his term of office, President Lincoln held the then prevailing belief in the supremacy of the States in all matters not directly under federal control, and as a matter of course believed that at the cessation of hostilities each State should immediately resume its old relations to the government, its local matters untouched by the central

---

[1] *Senate Journal*, 3d Session, 37th Congress, p. 24.

[2] See Pollard's *Lost Cause Regained*, pp. 44–57, for a discussion of the growth of Southern sentiment favoring measures of peace.

administration.[1] But the ability of Lincoln to modify his own beliefs on any subject as his experience widened was never better manifested than on this very question, and had he lived to control the administration through the period of reconstruction, it is not unreasonable to suppose that his attitude would have undergone still greater change. As the magnitude of the struggle became more apparent, he began to deliberate upon the advisability of striking at the root of the evil, despite the blow it struck at state liberty, and the two proclamations of September 22, 1862, and January 1, 1863,[2] mark the basis of the executive plan of reconstruction. The Pierpoint government of Virginia had been recognized in 1861, but its recognition was in harmony with the early attitude of Congress towards the States, and involved no questions which could show a distinct executive policy.

In 1862, after the capture of New Orleans, a military governor of Louisiana was appointed, many persons in the vicinity of New Orleans were enrolled as citizens of the United States, and two districts elected representatives to Congress, under the provisions of the old state constitution.[3] In this case there was a distinct development of the executive policy. Here was a military governor, appointed by the President and so an instrument of the Executive, interfering with the civil government of the State, controlling elections, deciding what districts were entitled to elections, and fixing the date of election. This was very different from simple restoration, with its theory that the national government must in no way interfere with the State govern-

---

[1] It is improbable that he ever modified his views as to the continued existence of the States—views which were essentially those of his successor, though less dogmatically asserted. See Hurd, *Theory of Our National Existence*, 36 and *Index;* Pollard, *Lost Cause Regained*, 65.

[2] Cooper, *American Politics*, pp. 141–3.

[3] Blaine, *Twenty Years of Congress*, ii, 36.

ments. And when the two members elect, Messrs. Flanders and Hahn, presented themselves for admission into the House of Representatives, the Democrats, consistently with their belief in restoration, which up to that time had met with no serious opposition, opposed their admission strongly. In the discussion which arose, Mr. Voorhees well expressed the difference in theory between the Democratic view and that which was ultimately to be adopted. The problem was stated by him as follows:[1] "If the Southern Confederacy is a foreign power, an independent nationality to-day, and you have conquered back the territory of Louisiana, you may then substitute a new system of laws in the place of the laws of that State. You may then supplant her civil institutions by institutions made anew for her by the proper authority of this *Government*—not by the executive, but by the *legislative* branch of the Government, assisted by the Executive simply to the extent of signing his name to the bills of legislation." "But if the theory we have been proceeding upon here, that this Union is unbroken; that no States have sundered the bonds that bind us together; that no successful disunion has yet taken place—if that theory is still to prevail in these halls, then this can not be done. You are as much bound to uphold the laws of Louisiana in all their extent and in all their parts, as you are to uphold the laws of Pennsylvania or New York, or any other State whose civil policy has not been disturbed."

The strong appeal to remain true to the theory first maintained by Congress, did not succeed in shutting the Louisianians out, and for one month, February to March, 1863, they were recognized as members. The later refusal to admit members from insurrectionary States was due, not to a supposed inconsistency with restoration proper, but to dislike of the presidential policy.

[1] *Congressional Globe*, 3d Session, 37th Congress, part i, p. 834.

And now with emancipation still another element entered into the question, and in the future reconstruction, Congress was of necessity forced to follow to a certain extent a new path laid out by the President. A State after January, 1863, in order to resume its former relations, must at least make one change in its institutions, and perfect restoration could no longer be considered. True, a large minority opposed the emancipation policy of the President, and their discontent took expression in resolutions such as Mr. Conway introduced into the House on December 15, 1862, in which he says that " the seceded States can only be put down, if at all, by being regarded as out of constitutional relations with the Union," implying, of course, the inability of the President to extinguish their local institutions. But such resolutions were never considered, while resolutions endorsing the policy of the President were agreed to.[1]

The next step in the development of the President's policy was the formation of a definite program, which States wishing to be restored to equal rights with the loyal States should follow. This plan of reconstruction, called by him at a later period the " Louisiana plan," was officially announced by the proclamation of December 8, 1863, and the annual message to Congress of the same date defended the stand taken.[2] This proclamation granted amnesty to all citizens (excepting certain specified classes [3]) who would take an

[1] *House Journal*, 3d Session, 37th Congress, pp. 69, 70.

[2] Cooper, *American Politics*, bk. i, pp. 141-3. On Lincoln's plan of Reconstruction, *Cf.* Gillet, *Democracy in the United States*, pp. 297-9; Pollard, *Lost Cause Regained*, 65, which claims that Lincoln could have successfully carried out his policy had he lived, but does not sustain the statement; Cox, *Three Decades*, etc., pp. 336-345; Wilson, *Rise and Fall of the Slave Power*, iii, 519-20; Scott, *Reconstruction during the Civil War*, 267 ff.

[3] These excepted classes were: (1) Confederate civil and diplomatic officers; (2) Confederates who had left U. S. judicial positions; (3) officers above colonel in army and lieutenant in navy; (4) those who had formerly been U. S. Con-

oath to support the Constitution, as well as all acts of Congress and proclamations of the President relating to slaves; and declared that whenever one-tenth of the voters of any insurrectionary State should take the oath, and re-establish their state government, " which shall be republican, and in no wise contravening said oath," that government would be recognized as the true government of the State and would receive the protection guaranteed to the States. But all questions concerning admission to Congress would, in accordance with the provisions of the Constitution, rest entirely with the respective houses of Congress. The questions of negro suffrage and federal supervision of the freedmen were not touched, and no provision was made to ensure good faith in reconstruction, beyond the mere oath exacted, and the general oversight of the President.

5. Under the provisions of the proclamation, three States, Louisiana, Arkansas, and Tennessee,[1] set up new governments, which were recognized by the President as true governments.[2] Congress, however, was by no means satisfied with this lenient way of treating the humbled States. The feeling that the executive was encroaching upon the legislative power added strength to the discontent. Many thought that if the presidential policy, without modification, were carried out, the reconstructed States would speedily revert to the control of the very element against whom the war had been waged. The House, by a strict party vote,[3] authorized the appointment of a select commit-

gressmen and had aided the rebellion; (5) those who left U. S. Army and Navy to aid the rebellion; (6) those who had treated negroes captured while in U. S. military or naval service otherwise than as prisoners of war.

[1] Wilson, *Rise and Fall of the Slave Power in America*, iii, 531–41; *Cf.* Gillet, *Democracy in the United States*, pp. 304–7.

[2] For results of this reorganization in Tennessee, see chap. iii.

[3] With one exception—a Republican, Whaley, of West Virginia, voted with the negative.

tee of nine, to consider that portion of the President's message relating to reconstruction, with authority to report by bill or otherwise. Henry Winter Davis was appointed chairman. Resolutions were submitted by Mr. Williams on March 14, 1864, which were backed by a sentiment in Congress that was of great significance. Congress began to feel its way towards a distinctive policy, which had heretofore been supported by only a few, who were considered as holding extremely wild and untenable views. These resolutions stated that although the local laws were subverted, and the functions of the civil authorities suspended in the States under armed occupation, "as soon as the rebellion is suppressed in any of the revolting States," the President should communicate the fact to *Congress,* "in order that it may take the proper measures for the reorganization of the civil governments and the re-establishment of the civil functionaries therein, and prescribe such terms as it may deem wise and proper and consistent with the public safety for the readmission of those districts as States of this Union." The exclusive right of the legislative power "to say upon what terms those territories shall be allowed to return to the Union," was also asserted.

The issue between Congress and the President took more definite form through the Davis-Wade bill of 1864.[1] This bill had been drafted during the latter part of 1863 by the select committee of nine, but it did not come before the House for consideration till March 22, 1864.

The objections of those who supported this bill to the Presidential plan, are clearly expressed in the speech of H. Winter Davis, in support of his measure. He says[2] that

---

[1] So called from the chairmen of the House and Senate committees reporting the bill.

[2] *Congressional Globe,* appendix, 1st Session, 38th Congress, p. 84. See also

it (the Presidential plan), "proposed no guardianship of the United States over the reorganization of the governments, no law to prescribe who shall vote, no civil functionaries to see that the law is faithfully executed, no supervising authority to control and judge of the elections. But if, in any manner, by the toleration of martial law lately proclaimed the fundamental law, under the dictation of any military authority, or under the prescriptions of a provost marshal, something in the form of a government shall be presented, represented to rest on the votes of one-tenth of the population, the President will recognize that, provided it does not *contravene* the proclamation of freedom and the laws of Congress; and to secure that, an oath is exacted." This government "may be recognized by the military power and may not be recognized by the civil power, so that it would have a doubtful existence, half civil and half military, neither a temporary government by law of Congress, nor a state government, something as unknown to the Constitution as the rebel government that refuses to recognize it."

In place of this method of organization, which Mr. Davis justly thought so wretchedly loose, he proposed that the President should appoint provisional governors over these States, whose first duty should be to enroll the white citizens, through duly appointed United States marshals. Then when a majority of these citizens should have taken the oath of allegiance, they should be permitted to hold a State convention for the purpose of forming a constitution under which the government might be re-established. But all Confederate office-holders and those voluntarily bearing arms against the United States were to be ineligible as delegates to the convention. The bill further provided that the consti-

Lalor, iii, 546: Cox, *Three Decades*, etc., 339–341; Wilson, *Rise and Fall of the Slave Power in America*, iii, 520-28; Johnson's *American Orations*, iii, 242–260; Scott, *Reconstruction during the Civil War*, 274 ff.

tution should "repudiate the rebel debt, abolish slavery, and prohibit the higher military and civil officers from voting for or serving as governors or members of the legislature." When these conditions should have been fulfilled, and the assent of Congress to the recognition of the new government obtained, the President should be notified, and should then officially recognize the government by proclamation, after which senators and representatives would be admitted to Congress.[1]

In the speech mentioned above, Mr. Davis claimed that "the bill challenges the support of all who consider slavery the cause of the rebellion, and that in it the embers of rebellion will always smoulder; of those who think that freedom and permanent peace are inseparable, and who are determined, so far as their constitutional authority will allow them, to secure these fruits by adequate legislation."

But in this plan there was no attempt to introduce negro suffrage. The only question of importance seemed to be: "How can we ensure the subservience of these States to the federal constitution?" The supporters of the Davis plan insisted that "the rebel States must be governed by Congress till they submit and form a state government under the Constitution"; otherwise "Congress must recognize state governments which do not recognize either Congress or the Constitution of the United States; or there must be an entire absence of all government in the rebel States; and that is anarchy." It was absurd, the argument continued, to recognize a government which did not recognize the Constitution; and "to accept the alternative of anarchy as the constitutional condition of a State is to assert the failure of the Constitution and the end of republican government. Until, therefore, Congress recognize a state government, organized under its auspices, there is no government in the rebel

[1] Cooper, *American Politics*, bk. i, p. 169.

States except the authority of Congress." From this it logically followed that in the absence of all State government it was the duty of Congress to "administer civil government until the people shall, under its guidance, submit to the Constitution of the United States," and reorganize government under whatever conditions Congress might require.

These arguments appealed to sentiments which were becoming very popular in Congress. The theory that a State by seceding ceased to exist as a State was gradually gaining ground, and the Davis plan, by which the central government was to control the State as a territory, though for so limited a time, rapidly gained supporters.

Mr. Fernando Beaman, of Michigan, who also considered that the seceded States had ceased to exist, said in an extended speech favoring the adoption of this bill:[1] "As a people without government or organization are in a state of anarchy, their efforts to establish law and order must be more or less impeded by caprice, by divided counsels, and by the want of forms, regulations, and methods. The passage of this bill is the establishment of incipient civil government, and provides at once rules, regulations and system, with the proper officials to carry them into execution."

Although the bill was avowedly drawn up to provide what the presidential plan failed to provide, a method of reconstruction so thorough that those elements which had produced the discord could no longer influence the state governments, it itself furnished no means to prevent any of these States from so amending their constitutions, after their senators and representatives had received recognition, that the very conditions of readmittance might be rendered nugatory.

But the bill seemed to the majority in Congress to offer a

---

[1] *Congressional Globe*, part ii, 38th Congress, 1st Session, p. 1246.

more practical plan than any yet propsed, and it passed the House May 4, by a vote of 73 to 59; the Senate, two months later, adopted it by a majority of four. But it failed to become a law by the adjournment of Congress before it received the President's signature.[1]

The President, in justification of his neglect to sign the bill, issued a proclamation on July 8.[2] This stated that while he was unprepared " to be inflexibly committed to any single plan of restoration," and also "unprepared to declare that the free State constitutions and governments already adopted and installed in Arkansas and Louisiana, shall be set aside and held for naught, thereby repelling and discouraging the loyal citizens who have set up the same as to further effort," nevertheless he was " fully satisfied with the system for restoration contained in the bill, as one very proper plan for the loyal people of any State choosing to adopt it," and that in such case when the people " shall have sufficiently returned to their obedience to the Constitution and laws of the United States," military governors would be appointed, "with directions to proceed according to the bill."

This attempt to modify the presidential plan virtually ended for the time the efforts of Congress towards the development of a distinctive theory, and the war thus closed with no well defined plan in operation, except that of President Lincoln, which was not well sustained by Congress. Only one thing seemed to be definitely decided. That was, that the seceded States, in whatever light they might be considered, were incapacitated from participating in presi-

---

[1] *Congressional Globe*, iii, p. 2106, 1st Session, 38th Congress.

[2] Cooper, *American Politics*, bk. i, 169–70. The President's action caused much dissatisfaction, Davis and Wade publishing a protest which impugned Lincoln's motives, declaring that he had committed an outrage on American legislation. See Johnson, in *Lalor*, iii. 5 and 6; Cox, *Three Decades*, etc., 341.

dential elections. A joint resolution to this effect was passed in 1865,[1] and in accordance with its provisions the electoral vote of Louisiana was ruled out.

Two men in the Republican party wielded the chief power in influencing that party to adopt the theory of reconstruction which was finally to prevail as the Congressional theory.[2] One was Thaddeus Stevens of Pennsylvania, and the other Charles Sumner, of Massachusetts. The latter was a recognized leader of the Senate, and his views concerning the mutual relations of the States in rebellion and the federal government were clearly expressed in a series of resolutions which he submitted February 11, 1862. These resolutions, although never brought forward for consideration, were printed, and coming from so influential a man had considerable influence in shaping the general attitude of Congress towards the question, and affected to some extent its future policy. They[3] were nine in number, with a well-worded preamble which put forward as a premise that " the extensive territory, thus usurped by these pretended governments, and organized into a hostile confederacy, belongs to the United States, as an inseparable part

[1] *Senate Journal*, 2d Session, 38th Congress, Feb. 8. Blaine (*Twenty Years of Congress*, ii, 46) explains that this joint resolution was intended as a rebuke to the President by the refusal of Congress to accept the proclamation of December 8, 1863, as a basis for the restoration of the States fulfilling its requirements. He then points out how Lincoln, with his usual tact, overthrows what triumph may have accrued to the leaders of the opposition by explaining that he " signed the joint resolution in deference to the view of Congress implied in its passage and presentation." His (Lincoln's) own opinion was that as a matter of course Congress had complete power to accept or reject electoral votes, and that the Executive had no right to interpose with a veto, whatever his own opinions might be. Blaine says that " his triumph was complete, both in the estimation of Congress and of the people."

[2] See Cox, *Three Decades of Federal Legislation*, 123; Johnston, in *Lalor*, iii, 54; Wilson (Woodrow), *Division and Reunion*, 261–2.

[3] *Senate Journal*, 2d Session, 37th Congress, pp. 194–6.

thereof, under the sanction of the Constitution, to be held in trust for the inhabitants in the present and future generations. * * * The Constitution, which is the supreme law of the land, cannot be displaced in its rightful operation within this territory, but must ever continue the supreme law thereof."

The first resolution declares that a vote of secession is void as against the Constitution, "and when sustained by force it becomes a practical *abdication* by the State of all rights under the Constitution, while the treason which it involves still further works an instant *forfeiture* of all those functions and powers essential to the continued existence of the State as a body politic, so that from that time forward, the territory falls under the exclusive jurisdiction of Congress as other territory, and the State being, according to the language of the law, *felo de se*, ceases to exist."

The second resolution denies the constitutional existence of the Confederate States. The third and fourth declare that the termination of a State terminates its peculiar local institutions, therefore slavery ceases to exist; and the fifth, sixth and seventh declare it necessary not to recognize or tolerate slavery. The eighth declares the obligation of the United States to protect all inhabitants, " without distinction of color or class." The ninth declares that Congress, in pursuance of the duties cast upon it by the total extinction of the States and by the constitutional obligation that the " United States shall guarantee to every State in this Union a republican form of government," [1] "will assume complete jurisdiction of such vacated territory where such unconstitutional and illegal things have been attempted, and will pro-

---

[1] The inconsistency in declaring a State to be extinct, and at the same time acknowledging the obligation to guarantee to it a republican form of government, is due to careless phraseology. Obviously Sumner uses the word " State," in these resolutions, where he means state governments.

ceed to establish therein republican forms of government under the Constitution; and in the execution of this trust will provide carefully for the protection of all the inhabitants thereof, for the security of families, the organization of labor, the encouragement of industry, and the welfare of society, and will in every way discharge the duties of a just, merciful, and paternal government."

Thaddeus Stevens, although recognized as one of the foremost men of the Republican party, advocated from the very commencement of hostilities views of so radical a nature, that he was looked upon by many as a fanatic. His influence accordingly worked in a different way from Sumner's. At no time did he consolidate his views into a series of resolutions, but upon every occasion where the subject could be touched upon, no matter how indirectly the topic might refer to it, he would state his theory of the relation of the seceded States to the Union. Persistently and consistently he advocated it; and he took pleasure in considering himself as in advance of his party, a prophet, pointing out the only right road, confident that sooner or later his party would see the wisdom of his policy and adopt it. Throughout those tempestuous years, his undaunted faith in the infallibility of his plan served to keep it constantly in mind, and attracted to him a constantly increasing number of followers, until at the beginning of the 39th Congress he obtained control, and became the recognized leader of his party in all matters relating to the Southern States. Though the plan of reconstruction as finally adopted contained many modifications, it was to a great extent the logical outgrowth of the Stevens theory. His whole theory rested upon the simple premise that wherever there is resistance to the Constitution, and that resistance cannot be overthrown without appeal to violent methods, there the Constitution is theoretically as well as practically suspended. As long as such resistance continues, the Constution remains suspended, and only the law-making and war-making power is able to determine when resistance has ceased. Consequently the federal government would have the undisputed right to treat the South as a conquered territory until there should be no question as to the safety of granting greater privileges. Those States had ceased to be States, consequently the "guarantee clause" had no application. Congress had unrestricted power over them, as simple territories of the federal government. On May 2, 1864, during the discussion of the bill to guarantee republican forms of government to the rebellious States, he declared that the rebellious States "were entitled to no rights under the Constitution and laws, which as to them were abrogated; that they could invoke the aid of neither in their behalf; that they could claim to be treated during the war as belligerents according to the laws of war and the law of nations; that they could claim no other rights than a foreign nation with whom we might be at war; and that they were subject to all the liabilities of such foreign belligerent," and that "the property of the morally and politically guilty should be taken for public use." [1]

[1] *Congressional Globe*, 1st Session, 38th Congress, part ii, p. 2041. See also his remarks on the Confiscation bill. Cox's *Three Decades of Federal Legislation*, pp. 365–374, contains a chapter on the policy of Stevens.

CHAPTER II.

1. We have briefly reviewed the theories that obtained greater or less consideration during the progress of the war, and have seen that no plan had been agreed upon by which the Southern States might resume their normal relations with the rest of the Union. Two or three States had, it is true, been nominally reconstructed under the provisions of the proclamation of December 8, 1863, but their good faith was strongly suspected, and their representatives were not able to secure recognition in Congress. The high personal esteem in which President Lincoln was held had prevented general demonstrations against his policy, but there was a wide-spread suspicion that he was inclined to deal too leniently with a people who had brought so much expense and misery upon the nation. The indignation of the North had increased with the progress of the war, and the belief that the South could be held in check only by the most stringent regulations and requirements was held by many.

2. So long as armed rebellion existed the question of reconstruction was a minor one, the attention of all being chiefly directed to the problem: " How can this rebellion be crushed out, and the South made thoroughly to realize that resistance is useless?" But when Andrew Johnson took the oath of office the rebellion was virtually a thing of the past, and the giant problem for the nation to solve during his administration was: " How shall we treat these conquered States

lying helpless, awaiting whatever fate may be allotted them?"
No other issue of importance served to offset it. The whole
nation was debating the question, and all were waiting to see
in what way the Executive would grapple with it.[1]

3. Those who feared that Lincoln had lacked sufficient firm-
ness and had been too tender hearted, believed that in Johnson the nation had as its Executive a man with correct convic-
tions and a strength of character which ensured both the
proper treatment of the South and the stability of the Union.
Johnson had an excellent record as military governor of
Tennessee, where his fearlessness and vigorous administration
had given him a reputation which brought to him the nomi-
nation of vice-president. From his severity to the rebels
while governor of Tennessee it was reasoned that he would
still remain severe and unyielding in his treatment of them
as President of the United States. He himself was always
fond of alluding to his past record as indicating his future
course. Thus, only six days after he took the oath of office,
he said while addressing a delegation of citizens of Indiana:[2]
"In reference to what my administration will be, while I
occupy my present position, I must refer you to the past.
You may look back to it as evidence of what my course will
be; * * * mine has been but one straightforward and un-
swerving course, and I see no reason now why I should de-
part from it. * * * My past is a better foreshadowing of my
future course than any other statement on paper that might
be made." Moreover, an examination of the speeches
made by him during the war shows the grounds on which
the people were justified in expecting a severe policy. An
extract from an address delivered in Nashville, June 9, 1864,
shows his views at that time as to who should carry on the

[1] See Wilson, *Rise and Fall of the Slave Power in America*, iii, 531–541.

[2] McPherson, *Reconstruction*, pp. 44 f. *Cf.* Wilson, *Rise and Fall of the Slave Power in America*, iii, 592.

work of reconstruction.[1] "In calling a convention to restore the State, who shall restore and re-establish it? Shall the man who gave his influence and his means to destroy the government * * * participate in the great work of reorganization? * * * Traitors should take a back seat in the work of restoration. If there be but five thousand men in Tennessee loyal to the Constitution, loyal to freedom, loyal to justice, these true and faithful men should control the work of reorganization and reformation absolutely." Later on in the same speech he said, referring to the traitor "born and reared among us :" " My judgment is that he should be subjected to a severe ordeal before he is restored to citizenship. A fellow who takes the oath merely to save his property, and denies the validity of the oath, is a perjured man, and not to be trusted."

4. Emphatic statements such as these, often repeated, insisting that the government of the States must be carefully kept in the hands of those whose loyalty was above suspicion, and advocating severe ordeals for those considered traitors, warranted the people of the nation in their faith in his extreme devotion to a strong Union. Yet soon after his inauguration a change in his attitude could be noticed. In his numerous speeches and interviews he shifts his ground, very gradually at first, but soon meeting the issue squarely, pledging himself to a policy which he faithfully carried into execution, and which the candid student must recognize as being thoroughly believed in by the President. Clemency towards the masses, but severity towards the leaders of the rebellion, was his attitude in his speech of April 21, above alluded to. He expressed his views as follows :[2] "It is not promulgating anything I have not heretofore said, to say that traitors must be made odious, that treason must be

[1] McPherson. pp. 46–7.

[2] McPherson, 44 ff; Moore, *Life and Speeches of Andrew Johnson*, 481 ff.

made odious, that traitors must be punished and impoverished. They must not only be punished, but their social
power must be destroyed. If not, they will still maintain an
ascendency, and may again become numerous and powerful;
for, in the words of a former senator of the United States,
' when traitors become numerous enough, treason becomes
respectable.' And I say that, after making treason odious,
every Union man and the Government should be remuner-
ated out of the pockets of those who have inflicted this
great suffering upon the country. But do not understand
me as saying this in a spirit of anger, for, if I understand my
own heart, the reverse is the case ; and while I say that the
penalties of the law, in a stern and inflexible manner, should
be executed upon conscious, intelligent and influential
traitors—the leaders, who have deceived thousands upon
thousands of laboring men who have been drawn into this
rebellion—and while I say, as to the leaders, punishment, I
also say leniency, concilation and amnesty to the thousands
whom they have misled and deceived.''

As Johnson said, he promulgated nothing new in this
statement of his beliefs regarding the treatment of the South,
save possibly a more definite affirmation of clemency to the
masses. In the Nashville speech of June 9, 1864, he had
still more emphatically urged extreme measures towards
the leaders.[1] " Treason must be made odious, and traitors
must be punished and impoverished. Their great planta-
tions must be seized and divided into small farms, and sold
to honest, industrious men. The day for protecting the
lands and negroes of these authors of the rebellion is past."
Again on April 24, 1865, in an interview with a number
of Virginia refugees, he reiterated the necessity of severity.
In this case, perhaps owing to the nature of the interview,
and the character of those to whom he was speaking, he

[1] McPherson, p. 47.

makes no distinction between the leaders and their followers, his definition of treason apparently including all soldiers and their abettors. In it he says:[1] " It is time that our people were taught that treason is a crime, not a mere political difference, not a mere contest between two parties, in which one succeeded and the other simply failed. They must know it is treason; for if they had succeeded, the life of the nation would have been reft from it, the Union would have been destroyed. Surely the Constitution sufficiently defines treason. It consists in levying war against the United States, and in giving their enemies aid and comfort."

The great liberality with which, beginning with the following month, the President used the pardoning power, and the extreme leniency with which all the leaders were treated, were in striking contrast with these sentiments. A situation was presented for Johnson to meet as President, which necessitated modifications of views held by him as governor. His attitude towards the leaders must be admitted to have undergone actual modification, notwithstanding his claim a few months later that he simply wished to make the leaders sue for pardon and realize the enormity of their offence.

5. The real secret of the apparently strange development of his policy, which we are about to trace out, lies in the fact that although at this time nominally a Republican, he was in reality a strict constructionist. He had always been a Democrat, and still held Democratic views. Only when secession began to be urged by the southern branch of the Democracy, did he break loose from his old ties. Accustomed to interpret the Constitution from a strict constructionist standpoint, accustomed to the belief that the power of the State was restricted only by the specific limitations of the Constitution, and that the federal government could exercise no power beyond that expressly granted it,

[1] McPherson, pp. 47–8.

he naturally treated the question of reconstruction from the
same standpoint. The surprising thing in Johnson's career
is the fact that in spite of his strict construction views, he
was strongly opposed to secession. He was therefore not
strictly logical. The extreme strict constructionist claimed
that the fact that the Constitution did not forbid a State from
seceding, made secession constitutional. But Johnson's love
for the Union was too great to permit him to carry his
strict construction views to such an extreme. On the contrary, the fact that the Constitution offered no way for a
State to secede from the Union proved to him that secession
was unconstitutional, and he looked upon that fact as one of
the greatest safeguards for the protection of the Commonwealth.[1] To his mind it logically followed that because
secession was unconstitutional, it was absolutely impossible
for a State to secede, and therefore equally impossible for a
State to commit treason. Individuals might commit treason
and be punished therefor, but States never. However
strongly at any time he may have urged the punishment of
traitors, he never argued for or believed in the abrogation of
any of the State's privileges. His reputation for belief in
severity was based entirely upon severity on individuals.
"Make treason odious" was his favorite expression, but
always used in a concrete sense.[2]

[1] See Gillett, *Democ. in the U. S.*, pp. 333–337, for a discussion of Johnson's
policy and mistakes from the Democratic standpoint.

[2] Mr. Blaine in his *Twenty Years of Congress*, vol. ii, pp. 63–70, ascribes the
apparently great modification of Johnson's attitude towards the South to two
causes: First, the personal influence of Seward; second, the flattery of Southern
leaders. He assumes Johnson to have been thoroughly determined to carry out
a harsh policy of reconstruction, and points out that of the six members of the
Cabinet, excluding Mr. Seward, three were radical and three conservative in their
views, offsetting each other in their influence upon Johnson. He then calls
attention to the fact that Mr. Seward's most conspicuous faculty was the power to
convince listeners against their will through his personal conversation with them.
With this remarkable faculty he believes Mr. Seward to have deliberately settled

6. After his accession to the Presidency, the only modification of his policy was an increased clemency to the conquered rebel. This can be accounted for easily as the natural result of actual contact with the problem. Rhetorically to assert that all traitors must be punished is one thing—to apply the punishment is another. Then Johnson's most able advisers approved his attitude and urged even greater moderation. Finally, his firm faith in the success of his provisional governments persuaded him to a still more liberal use of the pardoning power, while the growing opposition of Congress added the element of stubbornness to the complication. But, the true explanation of the change is to be found in his general constitutional views.

So early as April 21 he frankly states his position. In

down to the task of reversing the President's views as to reconstruction. " Equipped with these rare endowments," he says, " it is not strange that Mr. Seward made a deep impression upon the mind of the President. In conflicts of opinion the superior mind, the subtle address, the fixed purpose, the gentle yet strong will, must in the end prevail." Mr. Seward's fervent pleadings, Blaine thinks, caused a marked change in Johnson's beliefs, and inclined him to look favorably upon the glory of a merciful, lenient administration. The leaders in the South, quickly noticing the change in Johnson's attitude, took advantage of the opportunity, and by judicious flattery completed the work which Seward had begun, and placed Johnson before the world as the ardent champion of immediate restoration. The theory impresses one with its apparent reasonableness, but as Mr. Blaine produces no evidence beyond his own authority, one is inclined to look upon it as an ingenious explanation based upon the environment of Johnson. Doubtless Seward presented his view on the situation with his accustomed ability, and probably it influenced Johnson's view to a certain extent. The second part of the supposition can also readily be granted—that the vanity of Johnson was played upon by those whose flattery was most pleasing to one who had sprung from the ranks of those accustomed to be dictated to and spurned by these same men. Yet to ascribe the adoption of so important a policy, affecting all the fundamental principles upon which strict and loose constructionists are divided, to these influences, appears to be a superficial judgment based upon opinions formed in the heat of the struggle, when extraneous influences are always given undue prominence by the participants. The whole career of Johnson proves the logical exactness with which he followed strict construction dogma in all points excepting the doctrine of secession.

his speech on that day he says: "Provision" (in the Constitution) "is made for the admission of new States; no provision is made for the secession of old ones. * * * The Government is composed of parts, each essential to the whole, and the whole essential to each part."[1] He emphatically urges that the Constitution provides a panacea for rebellion. "The United States (that is, the great integer) shall guarantee to each State (the integers composing the whole) in this Union a republican form of government. Yes, if rebellion has been rampant, and set aside the machinery of a State for a time, there stands the great law to remove the paralysis and revitalize it, and put it on its feet again." He also harmonizes his strict construction views with the fact of emancipation. "A State may be in the Government with a peculiar institution, and by the operation of rebellion lose that feature; but it was a State when it went into rebellion, and when it comes out without the institution it is still a State."

President Johnson did not allow many days to pass by after his installation, before he began to give practical evidence of his attitude towards the conquered South.[2] The first step which he made was an order, issued April 29, re-

---

[1] McPherson, *Hist. of Recon.*, 45, 46.

[2] The repudiation of the Sherman-Johnston agreement of April 18th was of a negative character, and did not commit the administration to any policy. Coming, as it did, so shortly after his inauguration, it was taken by those expecting harsh measures from the President as an indication of such a policy. An examination of the circumstances, however, shows that Johnson was merely following the policy supposed to have been adopted by Lincoln, and evidenced by instructions sent to Grant on March 3 in regard to a proposed conference with Lee. Stephens' charge (*War between the States*, ii, 632), that Johnson was bound to ratify the agreement as consistent with the Crittenden Resolution of 1861, is inadmissible. Generals in the field manifestly have no right to decide momentous political questions. For a copy of the Sherman-Johnston agreement, and the official dispatch giving particulars of its disapproval, see McPherson, *Hist. of Recon.*, 121–2.

storing partial commercial intercourse to that portion of the Confederate States lying east of the Mississippi river and within the lines of national military occupation. This removed at the outset one of the chief burdens that had resulted from the insurrection, and would he thought act powerfully in the restoration of peaceful pursuits in that section. The following August another proclamation removed all remaining restrictions on trade in those States, declaring that all necessity for restriction had ceased.[1]

On May 9, 1865, the order restoring the administration of the United States in the State of Virginia was issued.[2] It authorized the Secretary of the Treasury to nominate assessors of taxes, collectors of customs, and other officers of the Treasury Department, and further provided that in making appointments the preference should be given to " qualified loyal persons residing within the districts where their respective duties are to be performed. But if suitable persons shall not be found residents of the districts, then persons residing in other States or districts shall be appointed." Post offices and post routes were to be established, and district judges empowered to hold courts, while " to carry into effect the guarantee of the Federal Constitution of a republican form of state government, * * * Francis H. Pierpoint, Governor of the State of Virginia, will be aided by the Federal Government," in his administration of the state government, in whatever way might be necessary.

The Amnesty Proclamation was issued on May 29, and was in effect a renewal of the provisions of Lincoln's proclamation of December 8, 1863, relating to amnesty; but it increased the number of classes excepted from the benefits of the proclamation, from seven to fourteen,[3] and provided

[1] McPherson, p. 13–14.

[2] McPherson, p. 8.

[3] See Appendix; Savage, *Life and Public Services of Andrew Johnson*, 370–373.

that special application for pardon might be made by any of
the excepted classes, to the President, who would exercise
liberal clemency. Inasmuch as the excepted classes included all those whom less than three weeks previously he
had been denouncing as traitors to be punished and impoverished, such great liberality, displayed in so short a
time, was somewhat surprising.[1] The proclamation further
empowered the Secretary of State to make all needful regulations for the administration and recording of the amnesty
oath ; and in accordance with this provision the Secretary of
State ordered that the oath might be taken before any commissioned officer of the United States, or before any civil or
military officer of a loyal State or Territory, who was legally
qualified to administer oaths.

On the same day that he issued the Amnesty Proclamation,
President Johnson appointed William W. Holden Provisional
Governor of North Carolina.[2] This was his first radical step
in the carrying out of his policy of reconstruction. The
order restoring the authority of the United States in Virginia was not of so great importance, as the State had
nominally been under the Pierpiont government since near
the beginning of the war, and the mere restoration of certain
United States officers in that State did not involve to any
extent the vital questions of the hour.[3] But with the appointment of Mr. Holden, and the instructions accompanying

[1] Blaine, ii, 70–76, ascribes this amnesty proclamation to the personal influence
of Mr. Seward, who favored all but the 13th excepted class (property holders
above $20,000). This certainly offers a good explanation of the promptness of
his action, and is not inconsistent with the theory of Johnson's attitude as outlined
above.

[2] McPherson, p. 11; Blaine, ii, 77, 78.

[3] Tennessee, of course, having been reorganized during Lincoln's administration, under the direction of Military Governor Johnson, cannot be considered in
connection with Johnson's policy as President. Louisiana and Arkansas also retained their reorganized governments until the reconstruction acts took effect.
See Blaine, ii, 79, 80.

the order of appointment, President Johnson unfolded, in its entirety, his theory.

The order declared that the rebellion, though now almost entirely overcome, had deprived the people of North Carolina of all civil government, and that accordingly the United States was constitutionally bound to secure to them a republican form of government. Therefore for the purpose of enabling the people to organize a government, he appointed William W. Holden Provisional Governor of North Carolina, whose duty it should be " at the earliest practicable period, to prescribe such rules and regulations as may be necessary and proper for convening a convention, composed of delegates to be chosen by that portion of the people of said State who are loyal to the United States, and no others, for the purpose of altering or amending the constitution thereof; and with authority to exercise, within the limits of said state, all the powers necessary and proper to enable such loyal people of the State of North Carolina to restore said State to its constitutional relations to the Federal government, and to present such a republican form of state government as will entitle the State to the guarantee of the United States therefor, and its people to protection by the United States against invasion, insurrection, and domestic violence," provided, however, that all electors should have previously taken the oath of allegiance, and should be voters according to the law of North Carolina in force previous to secession. The order further directed that the Provisional Governor should be aided by the military power in carrying out the proclamation. The other clauses were similar to clauses in the order re-establishing the authority of the United States in Virginia.

Similar proclamations were issued as follows : June 13, for Mississippi; June 17, for Georgia and Texas ; June 21, for Alabama; June 30, for South Carolina; July 13, for Florida.

Within three months after his inauguration, accordingly, Johnson had set the forces going throughout the South by which he hoped that peace and tranquillity might be established, and the Union once more become an undivided whole. In the execution of this most important work, he had not asked for the co-operation or advice of Congress. Confident of the correctness of his ideas, feeling sure that they were only the logical results of a true interpretation of the Constitution, he pursued his policy of reconstruction. In so doing he was also consistently following the path marked out by his predecessor. His plan was essentially that which Lincoln had advocated and attempted to carry into execution. But we have seen that even under a man enjoying such universal confidence as did Lincoln, the country viewed with distrust, and Congress openly resented, a policy which seemed to commit to a recently insurrectionary people the whole responsibility for proper reconstruction, requiring from them no surety for sincerity save an oath which all knew would be regarded by the majority as a mere form with little significance. The same policy when adopted by Johnson was naturally looked upon with still more suspicion.

Lincoln was a man of tact and judgment, who was capable of seeing and confessing a mistake, whose sole object was to do that which, all things being considered, should seem best for the Union.

Johnson, on the contrary, from his natural arbitrariness and narrowness, was a man who held most tenaciously to his views, had little consideration for the views of others, and who was always determined that his own way should be carried out. Under such circumstances it would have been little short of marvelous, had he been able to carry out a policy in itself disliked, without sooner or later coming into collision with those who disapproved his theory.

The provisional governors appointed were not slow in

carrying out the provisions of the proclamations, and conventions met in the various states as follows: Mississippi, August 14; Alabama, September 12; South Carolina, September 13; North Carolina, October 2; Georgia, October 25; Florida, October 25; and Texas in March, 1866. In all these conventions the secession ordinances were repealed, annulled or declared null and void,[1] and slavery was declared abolished. All but Mississippi and South Carolina repudiated the rebel debt, and all but Mississippi and Texas ratified the 13th Amendment.

Meanwhile Johnson made liberal use of the pardoning power, and large numbers of the excepted classes were thus restored to all the privileges of citizens of the United States. The reconstruction was very rapid; so rapid, as Johnson himself said, that he could scarcely realize it; "it appears like a dream."

The extreme similarity of this method of reconstruction to that advocated by the Democracy could not escape attention, and Democrats freely asserted that in his ideas the President was "going over to them." This, while to a certain extent true, for he was always a Democrat in principle, was vigorously denied by Johnson in an interview with Geo. L. Stearns on October 3, 1865. In it he claimed that the Democratic party, finding its own views untenable, was gradually coming to adopt his principles, which he reasserted in the following form: "The States are in the Union, which is one and indivisible. Individuals tried to carry them out, but did not succeed, as a man may try to cut his throat and be prevented by the bystanders; and you can not say he cut his throat because he tried to do it. * * * Now we want to reconstruct the state governments, and have the power to do it. The state institutions are prostrated,

---

[1] The phraseology differed in the different States, depending upon the sensitiveness and pride of the legislature.

laid out on the ground, and they must be taken up and adapted to the progress of events; this cannot be done in a moment. * * * We must not be in too much of a hurry; it is better to let them reconstruct themselves than to force them to do it; for if they go wrong the power is in our hands, and we can check them in any stage, to the end, and oblige them to correct their errors; we must be patient with them. I did not expect to keep out all who were excluded from the amnesty, or even a large number of them; but I intended they should sue for pardon, and so realize the enormity of the crime they had committed."

7. Johnson realized that the sentiment in favor of negro suffrage was gaining great power in the North; and while feeling that pure manhood suffrage was undesirable and totally impracticable, because of the danger of thereby creating a "war of races," which he seemed constantly to fear, he determined to use his influence towards a gradual introduction of the suffrage. He would give the suffrage to negroes who had served in the army, to those who could read and write, and to those owning real estate to the value of two hundred and fifty dollars. He made suggestions of this nature in letters to Governor Starkey of Mississippi, and Governor Hahn of Louisiana.[1] By some such limited suffrage he hoped that the radical element in the North would be satisfied, while there could result no danger to those States in which the negro population predominated.

He had long believed that the apportionment of Representatives should be based on the number of qualified voters; while a member of the legislature of Tennessee he had moved that the apportionment in that State be so made; and in the interview with Mr. Stearns he said: "The apportionment is now fixed until 1872; before that time we might change the basis of representation from population to qualified voters,

[1] McPherson, *Reconst.*, 7, 8.

North as well as South, and, in due course of time, the
States, *without regard* to color, might extend the elective
franchise to all who possessed certain mental, moral or such
other qualifications as might be determined by an enlight-
ened public judgment."[1]

But however desirable a limited suffrage might be, he insisted that the only safety for the nation lay in leaving the
whole subject to the discretion of the individual State.   The
only approach which he would make to national interference
would be through constitutional amendment.   In an interview with Senator Dixon of Connecticut, on January 28,
1866, he suggested that such an amendment might be worded
in the following manner :

"Representatives shall be apportioned among the several
States which may be included within this Union according to
the number of qualified voters in each State.

"Direct taxes shall be apportioned among the several
States which may be included within this Union according
to the value of all taxable property in each State.[2]

The great advantage of an amendment of this kind, in
President Johnson's opinion, was that Congress would thus
shift all responsibility regarding negro suffrage to the
States.   Each State would determine the qualifications for
voters, and its representation in Congress would depend
entirely upon the narrowness or broadness of the suffrage.

In the same interview with Senator Dixon, he described
the current contention over negro suffrage as "ill-timed,
uncalled for, and calculated to do great harm."

8. While the President was expressing his belief in qualified representation, and advising the States in process of
reconstruction to grant some form of limited suffrage, the
States themselves manifested no disposition to follow his
advice.   While he was describing them in October as lying

[1] McPherson, *Reconst.*, 49.   [2] *Ibid.*, 51–2.

helpless, they were busy framing laws which were aimed to counteract, so far as possible, the force of the emancipation proclamation.

When Georgia declared slavery abolished she did so with the proviso that " acquiescence in the action of the Government of the United States is not intended to operate as a relinquishment, or waiver, or estoppel of such claim for compensation of loss sustained by reason of the emancipation of his slaves, as any citizen of Georgia may hereafter make upon the justice and magnanimity of that Government." [1] Alabama, South Carolina, and Florida in their ratifications of the 13th Amendment stated their understanding to be that it did not confer upon Congress power to legislate upon the political status of the freedman. The Alabama legislature passed joint resolutions in which it was affirmed : " That Alabama will not voluntarily consent to change the adjustment of political power as fixed by the Constitution of the United States, and to constrain her to do so, in her present prostrate and helpless condition, with no voice in the councils of the nation, would be an unjustifiable breach of faith.[2]

But most important of all was the legislation of these States respecting the freedman. All were confronted by a host of emancipated blacks, whose legal status had to be determined. The legislatures had before them work of the most delicate nature, inasmuch as it not only vitally affected every person in their own section, but also attracted the keenest interest from the whole North. All realized that Johnson's policy would here undergo the crucial test. Would the legislators of these States, so soon thrown upon their own responsibility, show due consideration for the new order of things, or would they take advantage of their opportunity and proceed to draw the color line as sharply as ever, discriminating against the negro, and deny-

[1] McPherson, 20.	[2] *Ibid.*, 21–2.

ing him privileges which should be allowed him? Had the
South proved equal to the situation, the wisdom of Johnson's
policy would have been sustained, and the bitterness characteristic of the 39th and 40th Congresses would have been
avoided.

Mississippi was the first to adopt "black laws" obnoxious
to the North. Her vagrant act was passed November 24,
1865. This provided that freedmen found with no lawful
employment or business, or unlawfully assembling together,
should be deemed vagrants, and be fined and imprisoned at
the discretion of the court. A poll tax for a freedmen's pauper
'fund was to be levied on all freedmen, and should any fail
or refuse to pay, he was to be hired out by the sheriff to any
one who would pay the tax and costs, preference being given
to his former master. Two days later a civil rights act was
passed. This allowed freedmen to sue and be sued, implead
and be impleaded, and to own personal property, but added
the important proviso that the section should not be construed " to allow any freedman, free negro or mulatto to rent
or lease any lands or tenements, except in incorporated
towns or cities," where they should be controlled by the
corporate authorities. Intermarriage of a white with any
freedman, free negro or mulatto, should be punished by imprisonment in the state penitentiary for life. A laborer
quitting before expiration of term of service without good
cause, forfeited to his employer all wages for that year up to
the time of quitting. Any one was authorized to arrest and
return a deserting freedman, receiving therefor five dollars
reward and mileage, all costs to be paid from the wages of
the deserter. Any one persuading or attempting to persuade any freedman to desert his employer before his term
of service expired, was guilty of a misdemeanor, and liable
to a fine of not less than twenty-five and not more than two
hundred dollars, and if the offender attempted to persuade

the freedman to desert, with a view of employing him without the limits of the State, the fine was to be not less than
fifty nor more than five hundred dollars. While it was
made lawful for a freedman to charge a white man with a
criminal offence against his person or property, and .to
make all needful affidavits, a supplementary act passed
December 2 provided that where sufficient proof was made
before a court or jury that the arrest and trial had been
falsely or maliciously caused, the freedman should be fined,
and charged with all costs, and on failure to pay should
be hired out at public outcry for the shortest time necessary
to discharge the debt. An act passed November 29, among
other restrictions, forbade freedmen to carry any fire arms,
ammunition, dirk or bowie knife, under penalty, and declared
that a freedman exercising the functions of a minister of the
gospel, without a license from some regularly organized
church, should be guilty of a misdemeanor, and become
liable to an imprisonment not exceeding thirty days and to a
fine not exceeding one hundred dollars.

Similar laws were enacted in the other States, varying
slightly in severity of punishment. The labor contract act
of Louisiana, passed in December, is of especial interest as
an evidence of the systematic way in which the Southern
legislators hoped to mould the unwieldy mass of freedmen
into a docile set of serfs. All agricultural laborers were required by this act to make their contract for the ensuing
year before the tenth day of January; said contract to em-
brace the labor of the whole family. After the contract had
been agreed to, no laborer was to be allowed to "leave his
place of employment until the fulfillment of his contract, unless by consent of his employer, or on account of harsh
treatment, or breach of contract on the part of employer,"
under penalty of forfeiture of all wages to the time of leaving.
"Failing to obey reasonable orders, neglect of duty, and

leaving home without permission, will be deemed disobedience; impudence, swearing, or indecent language to or in
the presence of the employer, his family or agent, or quar-
reling or fighting with one another, shall be deemed disobedience. For any disobedience a fine of one dollar shall
be imposed upon the offender. For all lost time from work
hours, unless in case of sickness, the laborer shall be fined
twenty-five cents per hour. For all absence from home
without leave the laborer will be fined at the rate of two
dollars per day." [1]

The cruelty and injustice possible in the administration of
these acts is even greater than their casual perusal would indicate. Many of these acts, nominally applying to both races
with equal severity, were in reality intended to apply solely
to the negro. The vagrants always proved to be colored.
The acts purporting to secure the protection of the freedmen were cunningly hedged in by limitations which made
them worthless. The employer was made the sole judge of
the acts of his employees—a privilege which could not but
be flagrantly abused. Laws that made it almost impossible
for the freedman to secure the just return for his labor, were
followed by laws punishing him for his poverty. The fines
for his so-called offences were excessively severe, and the
punishments were almost always such as to reduce him to
slavery for limited terms. The whole system, taken advantage of as it could not fail to be where the dominant classes
were almost unanimously desirous to retain the negro in
subjection, resulted in his practical slavery during those
seasons of the year in which his labor was most needed,
and in utter neglect and lack of support when his labor was
not in demand.

9. Although the enactment of these stringent laws at this
time was a political mistake, and was fraught with most

[1] McPherson, 43; Blaine, ii, 102–3.

serious consequences for the South, it is proper to notice what was said in their justification. Many of them did not differ materially from similar statutes in the Northern States. Even some of the harshest laws, those which were received with wide-spread indignation throughout the North, could almost be duplicated by laws at that time in force in such States as Rhode Island and Connecticut. Even the phraseology, the using of the words master, mistress and servant, which was deemed objectionable and suggestive by Northern Republicans, could be found in Northern statutes.

The South felt confident that the negro was unable actively to assume the duties of citizenship. The Southern people feared, and with reason, that the immense mass of undeveloped humanity was liable to become turbulent and unmanageable, unless stringent laws could be framed which would hold it in check.[1] They were sincere in their statements that they believed that the interests of property, peace and good order demanded these laws. Unfortunately, the humanitarian ideas of the North harmonized too well with the political ideas of Congress. The enactment of the laws against the negro seemed to strike at the one and make possible the success of the other. The radical majority were quick to see their advantage, and did not hesitate to make the most of the opportunity. They assumed that the South deliberately intended to defy Northern sentiment, and ignored the possibility that the legislation in question was sincerely believed to be a necessary act of self-defense,

10. To Stevens and his followers the South had proved its impenitent condition, and had justified the most stringent measures of reconstruction. They declared that Johnson's policy had been fairly tested and that the results of the experiment were apparent. They argued that the South, em-

---

[1] See *Why the Solid South*, edited by Hilary A. Herbert, for a detailed presentation of the Southern view.

boldened by the conciliatory conduct of the President, was permitting the old rebel leaders to continue to wield the chief influence in affairs of state. The exclusion of these leaders from participation in the preliminary work of the reconstruction conventions was no check upon their influence in the State, and with the completion of reconstructon there was nothing to prevent them from occupying the chief state offices. What the President in the previous April had feared, was coming to pass, through his failure to do that which he had then said must be done—to make treason and traitors odious. In proof of the ascendency of the old elements, the highly questionable legislation of the South was cited, and the conviction of the Republican party that sterner measures were necessary was strengthened. As a natural result the doctrine of Thaddeus Stevens that the South should be regarded and governed as a conquered territory became practically the doctrine of the majority of Republicans, and Stevens became the leader of the House of Representatives. The year 1865 had made plain the necessities of the hour, the condition of the South, the attitude of the President, and in short had prepared the people for the great struggle which was to follow in the 39th and 40th Congresses.[1]

[1] The report of the Joint Committee on Reconstruction, June 18th (*House Reports*, No. 30, 1st Session, 39th Congress; McPherson, 84–93), gives a spirited summary of the action of the Southern States since the appointment of the provisional governors. See also Blaine, *Twenty Years of Congress*, ii, 84–107.

CHAPTER III.

THE ATTITUDE OF CONGRESS TOWARDS THE EXPERIMENT:
DEVELOPMENT OF THE CONGRESSIONAL THEORY.

1. The Thirty-ninth Congress began its labors on December 4, 1865, well aware that the President had separated himself from the Republican party so far that it was improbable that the executive and legislative departments would be able to work in harmony. The Democrats were beginning to commend the administration, and had even gone so far in some instances as to indicate, in resolutions passed in their state conventions, their approval of Johnson's plan of reconstruction. Republicans, on the other hand, were becoming quite reserved in their expressions of approval, and began to show a decided sentiment in favor of manhood suffrage as involving less danger and more benefit to the Republic than any plan which even partially excluded the negro from the franchise. The legislation of the Southern States had convinced many that without the negro vote there would be no way to keep the old insurrectionary element from completely monopolizing their state governments.[1]

Congress with its large Republican majorities[2] in both

[1] Lalor, iii, 546.

[2] Senate: Republicans, 40; Democrats, 11; House: Republicans, 145; Democrats, 40. The work before Congress was well expressed by Schuyler Colfax in his speech made upon taking the Speaker's chair. Speaking of Congress he said: "Representing, in its two branches, the States and the people, its first and highest obligation is to guarantee to every State a republican form of government. The rebellion having overthrown constitutional State governments in many States, it is

houses was expected to deal with the problem, correct the abuses which had arisen from the too lenient policy of the President, and inaugurate a policy which should bring about an equality of individual rights throughout the Union.

2. The calling of the roll by the clerk of the House, Edward McPherson, marked the commencement of active opposition to the presidential policy. All of the late insurrectionary States excepting Texas, whose convention did not meet until the following March, had elected senators and representatives. Their action in choosing or these and other high official positions members of the Confederate Congress, and civil and military officers of the Confederacy, was very unwise and did much to strengthen opposition to the recognition of these States.[1]

yours to mature and enact legislation which, with the concurrence of the Executive, shall establish them anew on such a basis of enduring justice as will guarantee all the necessary safeguards to the people, and afford what our Magna Charta, the Declaration of Independence, proclaims is the chief object of government—protection to all men in their inalienable rights. * * * * Then we may hope to see the vacant and once abandoned seats around us gradually filling up, until this hall shall contain representatives from every State and district; their hearts devoted to the Union for which they are to legislate, jealous of its honor, proud of its glory, watchful of its rights, and hostile to its enemies." *Congressional Globe*, 39th Congress, 1st Session, p. 5. See Blaine, *Twenty Years of Congress*, ii, 111, 112.

[1] Among the Senators elected were Alexander H. Stephens, Vice-President of the Confederacy, and H. V. Johnson, a Senator in the rebel Congress, both from Georgia; from North Carolina, W. A. Graham, Senator in the rebel Congress; from South Carolina, B. F. Perry, a Confederate States judge, and J. I. Manning, volunteer aid to General Beauregard at Fort Sumter and Manassas (McPherson, 106–7). Among the Representatives chosen were: from Alabama, Cullen A. Battle, a Confederate general, and T. J. Foster, a Representative in the rebel Congress; from Georgia, Philip Cook and W. T. Wofford, generals in the Confederate army; from Mississippi, A. E. Reynolds and R. A. Pinson, rebel colonels, and J. T. Harrison, in rebel provisional Congress; from North Carolina, Josiah Turner was a rebel colonel, and a member of the rebel Congress, and T. C. Fuller a rebel Congressman; from South Carolina, J. D. Kennedy was a colonel, and Samuel McGowan a general in the rebel army, and James Farrow, a rebel Congressman.

Louisiana, Arkansas and Tennessee, having been recognized by Lincoln as reconstructed, stood upon a somewhat different footing from the others, but in a caucus of the Republican members of the House, held previous to the organization of Congress, it had been decided to omit the names of their representatives from the rolls so as to reduce all to a common level, that no embarrassing distinctions might exist to hamper Congress in the adoption of whatever policy it chose.

In accordance with the instructions of the caucus, the clerk refused to call the names of these representatives elect. A lively discussion immediately arose, in which emphatic protest was made against forcing in this way a policy upon the House at a time when due deliberation could not be had. It was boldly asserted [1] that the clerk was acting merely as the tool of the Republican party, and the claim was also made that the resolutions about to be introduced by Mr. Stevens of Pennsylvania were another part of the general plan to commit the House to a quasi-condemnation of the President, and virtually nullify in advance the recommendations which it was supposed he would make. But protest was useless; the names were not placed upon the rolls, and the first roll-call gave evidence that active resistance to the President was determined upon.

The Senate was almost equally prompt in making public its determination to take the process of reconstruction out of the hands of the President. It is the custom in Congress to refrain from the consideration of questions of public importance until the President's message has been received. At the opening of this Congress no such courtesy was observed. Among the very first proceedings of the Senate after its organization was the introduction of three

[1] By Mr. Brooks, of New York. *Congressional Globe*, 39th Congress, 1st Session, pp. 3, 4.

series of resolutions by Sumner.[1] The first series was in reference to the Thirteenth Amendment, declaring it to have become a part of the Constitution without reference to the action of the late so-called Confederate States. Such States, the resolutions affirmed, should be required to ratify the Amendment as one of the conditions precedent to restoration. The second series related to the guarantees which should be required of the States prior to resuming their relations to the Union. These guarantees were five in number. First: "The complete re-establishment of loyalty, as shown by an honest recognition of the unity of the Republic, and the duty of allegiance to it at all times, without mental reservation or equivocation of any kind." Second: "The complete suppression of all oligarchical pretensions, and the complete enfranchisement of all citizens;" impartial justice, and equality before the law. Third: The repudiation of the rebel debt and the assumption of the proper proportion of the national debts and obligations. Fourth: "The organization of an educational system for the equal benefit of all, without distinction of color or race." Fifth: "The choice of citizens for office, whether State or National, of constant and undoubted loyalty, whose conduct and conversation shall give assurances of peace and reconciliation." The third series was declaratory of the duty of Congress to the loyal citizens in the rebel States. They, especially those who had served in the Union army and those excluded from the ballot at the time of secession, should have control of the conventions to be called for reorganizing the state governments. "No state law or state constitution can be set up as an impediment to the national power" in the reorganization of these States. No State recently in rebellion could be considered to have a republican form of government

[1] *Congressional Globe*, 1st Session, 39th Congress, p. 2; Blaine, *Twenty Years of Congress*, ii, 113–115.

"where the elective franchise and civil rights are denied to the Union soldier, his relatives, or the colored race."

The submission of these resolutions was of significance merely as a formal declaration that the President was to be ignored and an independent policy formed. The plan of reconstruction, as here presented, embodied many impracticabilities and impossibilities, but it indicated in broad outlines the propositions to be discussed in the succeeding months.

The House was still more active in its initiatory steps toward a policy. The resolution for the establishment of a, join tcommittee on reconstruction was introduced by Mr. Stevens at the first opportunity on the opening day, and immediately adopted. This resolution, after having been discussed in a Republican caucus,[1] was taken up for consideration in the Senate on December 12,[2] was made a concurrent resolution, that it might not need the approval of the President, and was passed with amendments. The debate on this resolution is of especial importance as the first formal test of the attitude of the individual Senators towards the administration. It brought out the fact that Senators Cowan of Pennsylvania, Dixon of Connecticut, and Doolittle of Wisconsin, would support the administration and oppose the congressional policy. Senator Norton, of Minnesota, soon joined their ranks, and Senator Lane,[3] of Kansas, broke from the party on the Civil Rights bill. The remaining Republican senators, while exhibiting natural differences of opinion, were united in their hostility to the existing method of restoration.

[1] Wilson, *History of Reconstruction*, 16 ff.

[2] *Congressional Globe*, 39th Congress, 1st Session, pp. 24–30.

[3] Senator Lane committed suicide on July 11, 1866. Mortification caused by abuse, as the result of his action, is supposed to have unbalanced him mentally. *Cf.*, Blaine, ii, 185.

The resolution, as amended and concurred in by the House, provided for a joint committee of fifteen, nine from the House and six from the Senate, "who shall inquire into the condition of the States which formed the so-called Confederate States of America, and report whether they or any of them are entitled to be represented in either House of Congress, with leave to report at any time by bill or otherwise."[1]

The appointment of this committee, with Thaddeus Stevens as a member, although Senator Fessenden of Maine was chairman, marks an important epoch in the history of reconstruction.[2]   Stevens, now the virtual leader of the House, represented a policy to which Johnson was thoroughly antagonistic, and from this time forth everything relating to the reconstruction of the Southern States was to be referred to this committee.   In addition, the committee took large masses of testimony from southerners, federal officers, and northerners travelling through the Southern States, in order that an intelligent judgment might be reached regarding the actual condition of these States.   The bills in which they embodied the results of their investigations constituted the basis of the final reconstruction.   The ill-defined

---

[1] The resolution as adopted by the House on the 4th contained in addition: "and until such report shall have been made, and finally acted upon by Congress, no member shall be received into either House from any of the so-called Confederate States, and all papers relating to the representation of the said States shall be referred to the said committee without debate." The Senate, however, considered such provisions to affect powers granted to each House separately, and which should not be entrusted to a joint committee. Therefore they were struck out, but on December 14 the House of Representatives passed resolutions binding itself to be governed by similar principles.

[2] The other members of the committee were: on the part of the Senate, Howard of Michigan, Grimes of Iowa, Harris of New York, Williams of Oregon, and Johnson of Maryland; on the part of the House, Washburne of Illinois, Morrill of Vermont, Grider of Kentucky, Bingham of Ohio, Conkling of New York, Boutwell of Massachusetts, Blow of Missouri, and Rogers of New Jersey.

sentiment of the Republicans, that the proper mode of dealing with the Southern States had not been found, was to be replaced by a vigorous policy which looked primarily to the proper protection of the freedman.

2. The message of the President, which was read on the 5th of December, had been eagerly awaited.[1] It had been expected that it would contain a decided statement of his exact views on reconstruction, and expectations were fulfilled. It was a clearly-written document, and outlined in extreme simplicity his attitude. In it he says, referring to the rebel States: "Whether the territory within the limits of those States should be held as conquered territory, under military authority emanating from the President as the head of the army, was the first question that presented itself for decision." His unhesitating answer to this question was that military rule was extremely undesirable, especially from the greatly increased powers which thereby would be held by the President. "The powers of patronage and rule * * * I could never, unless on occasions of great emergency, consent to exercise. * * * Besides, the policy of military rule over a conquered territory would have implied that the States whose inhabitants may have taken part in the rebellion, had, by the act of those inhabitants, ceased to exist. But the true theory is, that all pretended acts of secession were, from the beginning, null and void. The States cannot commit treason, nor screen the individual citizens who may have committed treason, any more than they can make valid treaties or engage in lawful commerce with any foreign power. The States attempting to secede placed themselves in a condition where their vitality was impaired, but not extinguished—their functions suspended, but not destroyed." These sentiments were but the repetition, in almost the same language, of sentiments previously expressed in various

[1] Blaine, *Twenty Years of Congress*, ii, 115.

interviews and speeches. The significance of the message was merely his recommitment to the policy he was applying in practice. But the consideration of the message in committee of the whole afforded a good opportunity for general discussions of reconstruction, which were continued at intervals throughout the whole session.

The great debate was opened on December 18 by Mr. Stevens, who reasserted his views, declaring that Congress has the sole power to receive back the States, the Executive concurring.[1] The States as States made war. "The idea that the States could not and did not make war because the Constitution forbids it, and that this must be treated as a war of individuals, is a very injurious fallacy. Individuals cannot make war. They may commit murder, but that is not war. Communities, societies, states, make war." He earnestly pleaded for negro suffrage both on grounds of expediency and of right, closing his speech with the oft-quoted sentence: "Sir, this doctrine of a white man's government is as atrocious as the infamous sentiment that damned the late Chief Justice to everlasting fame, and I fear, to everlasting fire."[2] Mr. Beaman, on February 24, after dwelling upon the horrors of the late war, said: "Those were sad, dark days, whose tinge was deepened by the frowns and hostile intrigues of foreign nations. But sadder still, and darker and more gloomy, will be that day in which the rebel States shall assume the control of our national government; when without guards or security for future good conduct, without protection to the blacks and loyal whites who have freely shed their blood in our defense, the seceded districts shall be declared recon-

---

[1] Wilson, *History of the Reconstruction Measures*, 42–105, contains a summary of the debates on reconstruction; see also Blaine, *Twenty Years of Congress*, ii, 128 ff.

[2] *Congressional Globe*, 39th Congress, 1stSession, pp. 72–5.

structed and restored States, and again launched upon their career of oppression, tyranny and crime."[1]

On March 10, Mr. Stevens made a speech upholding the right of the federal government to treat the conquered States in whatever manner was deemed advisable. " I trust yet to see our confiscation laws fully executed ; and then the malefactors will learn that what Congress has seized as enemy's property and invested in the United States, cannot be divested and returned to the conquered belligerent by the mere voice of the Executive. I hope to see the property of the subdued enemy pay the damages done to loyal men, North and South, and help to support the helpless, armless, mutilated soldiers who have been made wretched by this unholy war. I do not believe the action of the President is worth a farthing in releasing the property conquered from the enemy, from the appropriation made of it by Congress."[1]

Other speeches just as violent, condemning Johnson and his policy, were made during these general discussions. Thus Mr. Dumont of Indiana said : " Some gentlemen seem to be anxious to hear within this Hall the crack of the plantation whip, and to have a manifestation of plantation manners as in days of other years ; and as sure as God lives they will be abundantly gratified, if the policy of letting in the rebel States without guaranties shall prevail."[2] And Mr. Moulton, of

---

[1] *Congressional Globe*, 1st Session, 39th Congress, p. 1019.

[2] *Congressional Globe*, 1st Session, 39th Congress, p. 1309. These strong statements of the advisability of confiscation alarmed the Southern States greatly, and caused them to hate and fear Thaddeus Stevens. See Lalor, iii, 546 ff. The following extract from General Taylor's *Destruction and Reconstruction* (pp. 243-4), is characteristic of the Southern estimate of the man. General Taylor had occasion to call upon Stevens while endeavoring to get permission to visit Jefferson Davis, then in confinement at Fortress Monroe. He goes on to say : " Thaddeus Stevens received me with as much civility as he was capable of. Deformed in body and temper like Caliban, this was the Lord Hategood of the fair; but he was frankness itself. He wanted no restoration of the Union under the Constitution, which he called a worthless bit of old parchment. The white people

Illinois, a week later declared that " Andy Johnson will go
down to posterity, not only as the betrayer of his party, but
as an ingrate, infamous in all time to come to all honorable
men."[1]   In the same speech he says: "No rights of the
South that were lost by the rebellion were revived or repos-
sessed by traitors on the cessation of hostilities.   War destroys
all rights but the rights of war."[2]   Mr. Baldwin, of Massachusetts, described the attitude of the Southern States as follows:
" It is undeniably the aim of the old pro-slavery spirit to reduce them [the freedmen] to a condition as nearly like that of
slavery as circumstances will admit; a condition that would
yield all the advantages of slavery without any of its incum-
brances.   The hatred which has declared the freedom of
these people a calamity conspires diligently to make it so ;
the government is angrily forbidden to interfere with its
operations; and if there be an epithet of contumely and re-
proach that has not been hurled at those who would allow
these people the protection they need, it must be some
blackguard epithet not yet invented."[4]

But the policy of the President was not without its vigorous supporters, although they generally were found among
the Democrats.   Thus Voorhees, on January 9, eulogized

of the South ought never again to be trusted with power, for they would inevit-
ably unite with the Northern ' Copperheads ' and control the government. The
only sound policy was to confiscate the lands and divide them among the negroes,
to whom, sooner or later, suffrage must be given. Touching the matter in hand,
Johnson was a fool to have captured Davis, whom it would have been wiser to
assist in escaping. Nothing would be done with him, as the Executive had only
pluck enough to hang poor devils, such as Wirz and Mrs. Surratt. Had the
leading traitors been promptly strung up, well; but the time for that had passed.
(Here, I thought, he looked lovingly at my neck, as Petit André was wont to do
at those of his merry-go-rounds.)"

[1] *Congressional Globe*, 39th Congress, 1st Session, p. 1476.

[2] *Congressional Globe*, 39th Congress, 1st Session, p. 1616.

[3] *Ibid.*, p. 1617.

[4] *Ibid.*, p. 1828.

Johnson's policy as having "cleared away the wreck of a gigantic fraternal war, laid anew the foundation of government throughout an extent of country more vast than the most powerful kingdoms of Europe, revived confidence and hopes in the breasts of a despairing people, and won for its author the respect and admiration of the civilized nations of both hemispheres."[1] He also introduced a series of resolutions endorsing the policy of the President, and expressing confidence in him;[2] but these, together with an amendment by Bingham, expressing confidence that the President would co-operate with Congress, were referred to the Committee on Reconstruction, from which they were never reported.

Mr. Thornton, of Illinois, thought that "if those States are ever to be bound together in an equal and enduring union by us, we must rise to the high dignity of true manhood and Christian charity, and bury forever the feelings of distrust which now haunt the mind. The charge is constantly made that the Southern people are perfidious; that they will keep no pledges; that no oath will bind them. Can they accept your conditions precedent tendered in such a spirit? Never!"[3] Mr. Harding, of Kentucky, declared that the Republican party "with the cry of liberty on its tongue, is earnestly striving to subvert the foundations of republican government, laboring to centralize, consolidate and build up a frightful Federal despotism, under whose dark and deadly shadow self-government and all state rights would utterly sink and perish."[4]

4. The objectionable "black laws" of the Southern States, and the many tales of the oppression and cruel treatment of negroes, brought about a strong sentiment in

[1] *Congressional Globe*, 39th Congress, 1st Session, p. 155.

[2] *Ibid.*, p. 150.

[3] *Congressional Globe*, 39th Congress, 1st Session, p. 1169.

[4] *Ibid.*, p. 2256.

favor of legislation by Congress giving additional protection to the freedman.[1] The Act of March 3, 1865, had established in the War Department a "Bureau for the relief of Freedmen and Refugees," which was "to continue during the present war of rebellion, and for one year thereafter."[2] This bureau was to assume control of all abandoned or confiscated lands in the insurrectionary States, and to assign tracts not to exceed forty acres each to freedmen and refugees at an annual rent of not more than six per cent. of the value. The occupants were to be allowed to purchase the land at any time within three years. The bureau was also authorized to supervise all matters that might concern freedmen and refugees from any of the rebel States or from districts occupied by the army, and to furnish supplies to such as were in need.

To extend the powers of this bureau and to continue it in operation until affairs had resumed their normal course, appeared to be a practicable way to protect the emancipated race. A bill to this effect was introduced in the Senate by Mr. Trumbull on January 5, 1866,[3] and the Senate proceeded

[1] Gillet's *Democracy in the United States*, pp. 309–13, discusses the Freedmen's Bureau from the Northern Democratic standpoint.

[2] The first bill creating a Freedmen's Bureau was introduced in the House during the 37th Congress by Mr. Eliot, of Massachusetts, who during the 39th Congress was chairman of the Select Committee on Freedmen. It was not reported, but the same bill was presented in the first session of the 38th Congress, and passed the House by a vote of 69 to 67. It was returned from the Senate on June 30, 1864, amended so as to attach the Bureau to the Treasury Department. A committee of conference agreed upon a new bill creating a department of freedmen's affairs, reporting to the President. This passed the House, but failed in the Senate. The next attempt succeeded. *Congressional Globe*, 2d Session, 38th Congress, p. 1307. See Cox's *Three Decades of Federal Legislation* for an account of the Freedmen's Bureau; also Wilson, *Rise and Fall of the Slave Power in America*, iii, 472–485; Wilson (Woodrow), *Division and Reunion*, 263.

[3] *Congressional Globe*, 39th Congress, 1st Session, p. 1299. Mr. Doolittle on the 19th of December, 1865, had introduced a bill relative to the Bureau of Freedmen, but when reported from the Committee on Military Affairs, to which it had been referred, it was indefinitely postponed.

to its consideration on the 12th. With certain amendments the bill passed the Senate on the 25th by a vote of 37 to 10. The Select Committee on Freedmen[1] to which the Senate bill had been referred by the House, reported on January 30 a substitute bill. This passed the House on the 6th of February by a vote of 136 to 33; it was amended by the Senate on the 7th, the House concurring on the 9th. It was vetoed by the President on the 10th, and the Senate on the 20th attempted to pass the bill over the veto. The result showed 30 votes in favor, 19 against, less than a two-thirds majority, and the bill thus failed to become a law.[2]

The bill as presented to the President for his signature was entitled " An Act to amend an act entitled ' An act to establish a Bureau for the relief of Freedmen and Refugees,' and for other purposes."[3]   It continued in force the act of March 3, 1865, and extended the jurisdiction of the bureau to freedmen and refugees in all parts of the United States. The President was authorized to " divide the section of country containing such refugees and freedmen into districts, each containing one or more States, not to exceed twelve in number, and, by and with the consent of the Senate, appoint an assistant commissioner for each of said districts;" or in the discretion of the President "the bureau might be placed under

---

[1] This committee had been established by a resolution introduced by Mr. Eliot, of Massachusetts, on December 6, 1865. So much of the President's message as related to freedmen, and all papers relating to the same subject, were to be referred to it. The following were appointed members of the committee: T. D. Eliot of Massachusetts, W. D. Kelley of Pennsylvania, G. S. Orth of Indiana, J. A. Bingham of Ohio, Nelson Taylor of New York, B. F. Loan of Missouri, J. B. Grinnell of Iowa, H. E. Paine of Wisconsin, and S. S. Marshall of Illinois.

[2] Cox confuses this act with the act passed over the veto on July 16, declaring that it was passed over the veto on February 21. *Three Decades of Federal Legislation*, p. 444.

[3] See Wilson (Henry), *Rise and Fall of the Slave Power in America*, iii, 490–97; Wilson, *History of Reconstruction*, 148–184; Blaine, *Twenty Years of Congress*, ii, 164–170; Wilson (Woodrow), *Division and Reunion*, 264.

a commissioner and assistant commissioner to be detailed from the army." Districts when necessary were divided into sub-districts under agents. Military jurisdiction and protection were to extend over all connected with the bureau. Unoccupied public lands in the Southern Stases, not to exceed three million acres, were to be set apart for freedmen. Military protection was to be extended over all persons denied civil rights on account of race, color or previous servitude, and punishment was provided for those who deprived such parties of their civil rights.

The debates on this bill, occurring as they did before the President's speech of February 22, which will hereafter be noticed, lacked the great bitterness which was frequently manifested in the later days of the session. The fact that the veto message was received before the 22d accounts for the failure of the attempt to override it.[1]

The bill itself was moderate, the freedmen obviously needed the legislation, but the President considered the principles at stake of sufficient importance to justify him in further antagonizing Congress. His veto message cited a number of reasons for withholding the executive approval.[2] In the first place he claimed that there was no immediate necessity for the measure. Then it also contained provisions which were unconstitutional and unsuited to accomplish the desired end. His chief objection, of course, was based upon the continuance of military jurisdiction into a time of peace. This he declared clearly unconstitutional, a violation of the right of *habeas corpus* and of trial by jury; and he added that "for the sake of a more vigorous inter-

[1] *Congressional Globe,* 1st Session, 39th Congress. McPherson, *History of the Reconstruction,* pp. 73–4.

[2] The veto messages of the Presidents of the United States, from Washington to Cleveland, inclusive, have been compiled by Ben: Perley Poore by order of the Senate.

position in behalf of justice we are to take the risks of the
many acts of injustice that would necessarily follow from an
almost countless number of agents, * * * over whose deci-
sions there is to be no supervision or control by the federal
courts. * * * The country has returned or is returning to
a state of peace and industry, and the rebellion in in fact at
an end. The measure, therefore, seems to be as inconsistent
with the actual conditions of the country as it is at variance
with the Constitution of the United States."   He considered
the provisions which proposed to take away land from its
former owners without due process of law, unconstitutional.
Other more general objections were mentioned, such as the
immense patronage created and immense expense involved,
the dangerous concentration of power in the Executive, and
the ethical objection that legislation which implies that the
freedmen " are not expected to attain a self-sustaining condition must have a tendency injurious alike to their character
and their prospects." [1]

The unification of opposition to the President, which was
accomplished through his speech of February 22, afterwards
impelled the friends of the Freedmen's Bureau bill to make
another attempt to secure its passage, believing that it then
could be passed over the President's veto.[2]   The ball was
again set rolling by Mr Eliot, of Massachusetts, who on
May 22 introduced a bill designed to take the place of the
defeated bill, yet different enough to afford a plausible pre-
text for again bringing the question forward.   Slightly amended, it passed the House on May 29 by a vote of 96 to
32. The bill, with amendments, reported from the Committee
on Military Affairs, of which Senator Wilson, of Massachu-

[1] *Congressional Globe*, 39th Congress, 1st Session, pp. 915–917; McPherson,
History of Reconstruction, pp. 68–72.

[2] See Wilson, *Rise and Fall of the Slave Power in America*, iii. 497–99; Wilson, *History of the Reconstruction*, 184–195; Blaine, *Twenty Years of Congress*,
ii, 171–2.

setts, was chairman, was taken up for consideration by the Senate on June 26, and passed. The House non-concurring, a committee of conference was appointed, which made some minor changes, to which the Senate on July 2, and the House on July 3, agreed. A veto message of the President was received on July 16, and the bill was passed over the veto on the same day.[1]

To all intents and purposes this act differed but little from the first vetoed bill. It continued the original Freedmen's Bureau Act in force for two years, and contained certain additional provisions for the education of the freedmen, for the recognition of their civil rights, and for the protection of such rights by military power.

President Johnson, in his veto message, declared that a careful examination had convinced him that the same reasons assigned in his veto of February 19, applied also to this measure. Such legislation was justifiable only under the war power, and should not extend to times of peace. The now existing federal and state courts, he went on to say, were amply sufficient for the protection of the freedmen, and the existence of the prevalent disorders furnished no necessity for the extension of the bureau system. The practical operation of the bureau showed that it was becoming an instrument of fraud, corruption and oppression, while the civil rights bill, needless as it was, provided methods of protection far preferable to the military protection authorized by this bill. The legislation regarding the disposal of land was discriminating, unsafe, and unconstitutional, and in conclusion he urged upon Congress the dangers of class legislation.

[1] The votes were: House, 104 to 33; Senate, 33 to 12. For the text of the bill, see *Congressional Globe*, 1st Session, 39th Congress; McPherson, *History of the Reconstruction*, pp. 149–50. Blaine, *Twenty Years of Congress*, ii, 172, states that the bill was far less popular than the measure vetoed on February 19. "It required potent persuasion, re-enforced by the severest exercise of party discipline, to prevent a serious break in both Houses against the bill."

5. The mere veto of the first Freedmen's Bureau bill would not have been of great significance had it been the only act of the President at this time offensive to the rank and file of the Republican party. But on two other occasions he acted very indiscreetly, February 7 and February 22, the latter coming so shortly after the veto message on the first bill that the antagonism of Congress was greatly intensified.

On February 7, 1866, a delegation of colored representatives from fifteen States and the District of Columbia called upon President Johnson in order to present their wishes concerning the granting of suffrage to their race. Geo. T. Downing and Frederick Douglass acted as spokesmen. In reply, President Johnson described his sacrifices for the colored man, and went on to express his indignation at being arraigned by incompetent persons. Although he was willing to be the colored man's Moses, he was not willing " to adopt a policy which he believed would only result in the sacrifice of his [the colored man's] life and the shedding of his blood." The war was not waged for the suppression of slavery; "the abolition of slavery has come as an incident to the suppression of a great rebellion—as an incident, and as an incident we should give it the proper direction." He went on to state that the negro was unprepared for the ballot, and that there was danger of a race war. The States must decide for themselves on the question of the franchise. "Each community is better prepared to determine the depository of its political power than anybody else, and it is for the legislature * * * to say who shall vote, and not for the Congress of the United States."[1]

This plain statement of his opposition to negro suffrage greatly added to Johnson's unpopularity. This was not due to the fact that his views on that subject had not been made

[1] McPherson, *History of the Reconstruction*, 52–56.

public before, for he never had tried to conceal his attitude towards any of the questions before the people. But the attitude of the people themselves had greatly changed since the ill treatment of the freedmen and the objectionable legislation of the Southern States had been placed vividly before the public through the newspapers. The sentiment in favor of the extension of the franchise had rapidly gained strength; and the attitude of the President, made conspicuous anew by his almost harsh reply to so prominent a delegation representing such a wide extent of territory, called forth much hostile criticism, which, added to the vigorous letter published by the delegation in reply to the President, aided in unifying the opposition to him.

On February 22 he made a speech in which he not only attacked by name certain leading politicians, but also criticised in terms the legislative branch of the government. This speech marks a distinct epoch in the history of the struggle between the President and Congress. Prior to it, the latter, although conscious of the rapid divergence of the paths each was following, and determined to render as nugatory as possible the President's policy, had not permitted the feeling of personal antagonism to influence its actions to any great extent. But from this time forth the lines were sharply drawn, culminating in the impeachment. Johnson bitterly hated the Joint Committee on Reconstruction. The very manner in which it had been authorized— through a concurrent resolution instead of a joint resolution for the purpose of preventing executive action—had embittered him; the principles which its majority represented and the *personnel* of the committee were equally distasteful to him.

In connection with the speech of February 22, it should be noticed that Mr. Stevens had two days before introduced a concurrent resolution, which passed the House, providing

that no senators or representatives were to be admitted
until Congress should declare the State entitled to representation.   Such a provision, the practical effect of which would
be to place the subject in the exclusive control of the Joint
Committee on Reconstruction, Congress, as we have seen,
struck out of the resolution authorizing that committee's appointment.[1]   The President had good reason to believe that
Mr. Stevens' resolution would pass the Senate, as it did on the
2d of March, and he looked upon it as one more step in the
usurpation of power by an " irresponsible directory."   Sensitive to all tendencies towards centralization, he saw in the
power granted to the committee, and the measures proposed
by it, a tendency towards the conditions against which he
had spoken on April 21, 1865, when he said : "While I have
opposed dissolution and disintegration on the one hand, on
the other I am equally opposed to consolidation, or the
centralization of power in the hands of a few."

Public sentiment in Washington was very hostile to the
Freedmen's Bureau, and on February 22 a mass-meeting was
held to express popular approval of the action of the President in vetoing the bill.   Adjourning to the White House,
the crowd congratulated Johnson with tumultuous enthusiasm.
A man more cautious would have limited his reply to a tem-
perate expression of his views ; but Johnson, ever eager to
pose as the leader of the people, was led by the enthusiasm
of the moment to abandon himself entirely to his prejudices,
aggravated as they were by the circumstances above mentioned.   Thus, on the anniversary of Washington's birthday,
a day when he should have particularly refrained from par-

---

[1] *House Journal,* 39th Congress, 1st Session, 300, 315.   The resolution was
carried particularly to silence the Tennessee claimants for recognition.   The
somewhat anomalous position of that State gave grounds for the argument that
it should be classed in the same category with the other Southern States.   Thus
Mr. Stevens was able to get the power for the joint committee which he had
originally claimed.

tisan politics, he took occasion to assail the committee vio-
lentiy, declaring that the end of one rebellion was witnessing
the beginning of a new rebellion; saying that "there is an
attempt now to concentrate all power in the hands of a few
at the federal head, and thereby bring about a consolidation
of the Republic, which is equally objectionable with its
dissolution. * * * The substance of your government
may be taken away, while there is held out to you the form
and the shadow." He described the Joint Committee as an
"irresponsible central directory," which had assumed "nearly
all the powers of Congress," without "even consulting the
legislative and executive departments of the Government.
* * * Suppose I should name to you those whom I look
upon as being opposed to the fundamental principles of this
Government, and as laboring to destroy them. I say Thaddeus Stevens, of Pennsylvania; I say Charles Sumner, of
Massachusetts; I say Wendell Phillips, of Massachusetts."[1]

6. After the President had thus publicly stigmatized the
opponents of his policy as instigators of a new rebellion, and
classed Stevens, Sumner and Wendell Phillips as traitors to
be compared with Davis, there could be no hope of reconciliation, and the Republican party grimly settled down to
fight for its principles. The first important measure to take
effect was the civil rights bill.[2]

On the first day of the session Senator Wilson, of Massachusetts, had introduced a bill looking to the personal protection of the freedmen. It was aimed directly at the "black
laws" of the Southern States, and declared all laws, statutes,
acts, etc., of any description whatsoever, which caused any
inequality of civil rights, in consequence of race or color, to
be void. In his speech of December 13, 1865, explaining his

[1] McPherson, *History of the Reconstruction*, pp. 58–63.

[2] See Wilson, *Rise and Fall of the Slave Power in America*, iii, 684–692;
History of Reconstruction, 117–149; Blaine, *Twenty Years of Congress*, ii, 172–79.

reasons for introducing the bill, Wilson said that, while honest differences as to the expediency of negro suffrage might exist, he could not comprehend " how any humane, just and Christian man can, for a moment, permit the laws that are on the statute-books of the States in rebellion, and the laws that are now pending before their legislatures, to be executed upon men whom we have declared to be free. * * * To turn these freedmen over to the tender mercies of men who hate them for their fidelity to the country is a crime that will bring the judgment of heaven upon us." [1]

This bill and a similar bill introduced by the same senator on December 21, and one introduced by Senator Sumner on the first day of the session, never came to a vote, the last two being postponed indefinitely by the Senate. In place of these bills, Senator Trumbull of Illinois, chairman of the Committee on the Judiciary, on January 5, 1866, introduced a bill which, slightly amended, became a law. This measure passed the Senate on February 2, was amended and passed by the House on March 13, and the amendments were concurred in by the Senate on the 15th. It was returned to the Senate by the President, without his approval, March 27, and on April 6 the Senate passed the bill over the veto of the President by a vote of 33 to 15. Three days later the House passed the bill by a vote of 122 to 41, and the measure became a law.

As passed it was entitled, " An Act to protect all persons in the United States in their civil rights, and furnish the means of their vindication." It first declared " all persons born in the United States, and not subject to any foreign power, excluding Indians not taxed," to be citizens of the United States. Such citizens, without regard to race, color, or previous servitude, were declared to have the same rights in all the States and Territories, as white citizens, to make

[1] *Congressional Globe*, 1st Session, 39th Congress, pp. 39, 40.

and enforce contracts; to "sue, be parties, and give evidence; to inherit, purchase, lease, sell, hold, and convey real and personal property;" to enjoy the equal benefit of all laws for the security of person and property, and to be subject only to the same punishments. The second section provided penalties for the deprivation of equal rights. The third gave to the United States courts exclusive cognizance of all causes involving the denial of the rights secured by the first section. The remaining sections specified the powers and duties of the district attorneys, marshals, deputy marshals and special commissioners, in connection with the enforcement of the act, the ninth section providing: " It shall be lawful for the President of the United States, or such person as he may empower for that purpose, to employ such part of the land or naval forces of the United States, or of the militia, as shall be necessary to prevent the violation and enforce the due execution of the Act."[1]

From this summary of the act its nature can be seen plainly. Up to this time there had been no legislation affecting the *status* of the freedman. This declared him to be a citizen of the United States, and thereby entitled to all the privileges of citizenship. The war having resulted in the anomalous condition of the several millions of freedmen, some such legislation was necessary, especially in view of the fact that discriminative legislation was being enacted in the South. The bill was moderate in its terms, the most questionable portion being the section empowering the President to enforce the act through the war department, but even that in the then unsettled condition of the country had much to justify it.

The President's veto message was a lengthy document and discussed in detail the significance of the bill.[1] He

---

[1] *Congressional Globe*, 39th Congress, 1st Session, McPherson, *History of the Reconstruction*, pp. 75-8.

questioned the policy of conferring citizenship on four million blacks while eleven of the States were unrepresented in Congress. He doubted whether the negroes possessed the qualifications for citizenship, and thought that their proper protection did not require that they be made citizens, as civil rights were secured to them as they were, while the bill discriminated against the intelligent foreigner. Naturally, he also declared that the securing by federal law of equality of the races was an infringement upon state jurisdiction. " Hitherto, every subject embraced in the enumeration of rights contained in this bill has been considered as exclusively belonging to the States." The second section he thought to be of doubtful constitutionality and unnecessary, " as adequate judicial remedies could be adopted to secure the desired end, without invading the immunities of legislators, * * * without assailing the independence of the judiciary, * * * and without impairing the efficiency of ministerial officers. * * * The legislative department of the United States thus takes from the judicial department of the States the sacred and exclusive duty of judicial decision, and converts the State judge into a mere ministerial officer bound to decide according to the will of Congress." The third section he characterized as undoubtedly comprehending cases and authorizing the " exercise of powers that are not by the Constitution within the jurisdiction of the courts of the United States." He also considered the extraordinary powers of the numerous officials created by the act as jeopardizing the liberties of the people, and the provisions in regard to fees as liable to bring about persecution and fraud.

In addition to these objections he argued that the bill frustrated the natural adjustment between capital and labor

<hr />

[1] *Congressional Globe*, 39th Congress, 1st Session, pp. 1679–81; McPherson, *History of Reconstruction*, pp. 75–8.

in a way potent to cause discord. It was " an absorption and assumption of power by the General Government which, if acquiesced in, must sap and destroy our federative system of limited powers, and break down the barriers which preserve the rights of the States. * * * The tendency of the bill must be to resuscitate the spirit of rebellion, and to arrest the progress of those influences which are more closely drawing around the States the bonds of union and peace."

The next clash between the executive and legislative branches of the government was over the Colorado bill.[1] This bill provided for the admission of Colorado into the Union, and was passed May 3, being vetoed by the President on May 15, in accordance with the policy which he was endeavoring to carry out.[2] The nominal grounds, while strong in themselves, had less weight in Johnson's mind than the argument reserved for the final sentence of the message. This referred to the fact that eleven of the old States were unrepresented in Congress, and that it was in the " common interest of all the States, as well those represented as those unrepresented, that the integrity and harmony of the Union should be restored as completely as possible, so that all those who are expected to bear the burdens of the Federal Government shall be consulted concerning the admission of new States; and that in the mean time no new State shall be prematurely and unnecessarily admitted to a participation in the political power which the Federal Government wields." A second bill for the admission of Colorado was vetoed on January 29, 1867.[3] In the message President

[1] *Senate Journal,* 39th Congress, 1st Session, pp. 431–2; McPherson, *History of the Reconstruction,* pp. 82–3; Blaine, *Twenty Years of Congress,* ii, 275–80.

[2] McPherson, *History of the Reconstruction,* 81–2; *Congressional Globe,* 39th Congress, 1st Session, 2609.

[3] McPherson, 160–164.

Johnson stated that he could change none of his opinions expressed in the first veto, while he now saw many additional objections. Neither bill was passed over the veto. Another measure of like nature was the Nebraska bill, which was passed on July 27, the last day but one of the session. The President "pocketed" it. Both bills were again introduced at the beginning of the second session by Senator Wade, and the Nebraska bill was duly passed. It was vetoed January 30, 1867, but within ten days was passed over the veto by both houses, Nebraska being able to present stronger arguments for receiving statehood than Colorado, and consequently obtaining more support from the conservative members of the Republican party. The principal objection expressed in the veto message was the incongruities existing in the bill, the first section admitting the State "upon an equal footing with the original States in all respects whatsoever," and the third section providing that "there shall be no denial of the elective franchise, or of any other right, to any person by reason of race or color, except Indians not taxed." This assertion of the right of Congress to regulate the elective franchise the President declared clearly unconstitutional, and incompatible with an equal footing with the original States.[1]

7. The central event, naturally, of the first session of the 39th Congress was the report of the Joint Committee on Reconstruction. Although during the session there was a great amount of discussion as to the theory and method of reconstruction, and, as has been shown, two important measures were passed over the President's veto, the majority in the House still felt uncommitted as to the policy they should favor, excepting so far as the measures already reported from the committee had given shape to

[1] McPherson, *History of the Reconstruction*, pp. 164–6; *Congressional Globe*, 39th Congress, 1st Session.

their plans. A definite platform had not been erected on which they could stand, and they were not certain of the foundations on which to base constructive legislation. It was quite evident from the resolutions and bills reported from the committee to Congress, that the testimony taken before it had not changed the views of the majority of the committee, and the general tenor of the report was not a surprise to any one. Its constitutional importance cannot be questioned, since the Republican party adopted its construction of the Constitution, and proceeded to frame, on the lines marked out by the report, the bills which changed decidedly the relations between the States and the Federal Government, affording precedents for an extension of federal power which previous to the close of the war few could have been found to support.[1]

No theory as to the *status* of the Southern States was agreed on by the committee.[2] Among those signing the majority report several distinct views can be noted. The theory of Thaddeus Stevens, that the States were now merely conquered territory, at the mercy of the conqueror, has already been noticed. Mr. Boutwell, of Massachusetts, was one of those who theoretically differed from Mr. Stevens, preferring to consider the States as "dead States" within the Union. Mr. Bingham, of Ohio, was still less radical, simply calling them "disorganized States." But realizing the futility of introducing distinctions which could not affect the main question at issue, the majority dropped "the profitless abstraction," and agreed upon the general conclusions

---

[1] Hurd, in his *Theory of our National Existence*, p. 42, says that this report of the Joint Committee on Reconstruction " as being the most authoritative declaration of principles supposed to have been afterwards carried out in political action, is a document which, either for good or evil, will probably be regarded as one of the most important in the history of this country."

[2] For an extended discussion of the constitutional views of the members of the committee, see Hurd's *Theory*, etc., pp. 224 ff.

and recommendations. The report was finally presented to Congress on June 18, all the members signing excepting Johnson, Rogers and Grider, who submitted a minority report four days later.

The first portion of the report is a general review of the steps which had already been taken by the President, and of the powers of the executive and legislative departments. It was declared that at the close of the war the Confederate States were in a condition of utter exhaustion and complete anarchy. Congress having failed to provide for the contingency, the President had no power except to execute the national laws and establish "such a system of government as might be provided for by existing national statutes." These States "by withdrawing their representatives in Congress, by renouncing the privilege of representation, by organizing a separate government, and by levying war against the United States, destroyed their State constitutions in respect to the vital principle which connected their respective States with the Union and secured their federal relations; and nothing of these constitutions was left of which the United States were bound to take notice." The President had two alternatives: either to "assemble Congress and submit the whole matter to the law-making power," or to continue military supervision in his capacity as commander-in-chief of the army, until the regular assembling. Choosing the latter course, he appointed over the revolted States provisional governors who possessed military authority, but who "had no power to organize civil governments nor to exercise any authority except that which inhered in their own persons under their commissions." The President in his military capacity might properly permit the people to form local governments, execute local laws not inconsistent with national laws, and even withdraw military forces altogether if he deemed it safe. But to Congress,

not to the President, belonged the power " to decide upon
the nature or effect of any system of government which the
people of these States might see fit to adopt," and to fix
terms by which the States might be restored to all their
rights and privileges as States of the Union.   " The loss of
representation by the people of the insurrectionary States
was their own voluntary choice.   They might abandon their
privileges, but they could not escape their obligations," and
they could not complain.

None of the revolted States, the report continued, excepting perhaps Tennessee, were in a condition to resume
their former political relations.   Their so-called " amended
constitutions " had never been submitted to the people for
adoption, and when they were thus submitted there was
nothing to prevent their repudiation.   If these States were
without state governments, they should be regularly organized, but in no case had the proper preliminary steps
been taken.   The conventions assumed that the old constitutions were still in force, and that only such amendments
as the federal government required, were needed.   " In no
instance was regard paid to any other consideration than
obtaining   immediate   admission   to   Congress, under   the
barren form of an election in which no precautions were taken
to secure regularity of proceedings or the consent of the
people."   Before they were restored to their full rights
" they should exhibit in their acts something more than
unwilling submission to an unavoidable necessity."   Great
stress was laid upon the headstrong action of the States
since Johnson's proclamation of amnesty : the character
of the men elevated to the highest positions ; the discriminating legislation ; the arrogance of the Southern
press, and the opposition to the Freedmen's Bureau.   The
testimony of witnesses as to the general disposition to repudiate the national debt, if such a thing should prove

possible, and as to the natural reluctance to pay taxes, were perhaps too seriously taken, as was also the "proof of a condition of feeling hostile to the Union and dangerous to the government."

But, whether acting on exaggerated estimates or not, the majority of the committee formulated their conclusions into three clauses, which were as follows :

1. "That the States lately in rebellion were at the close of the war disorganized communities, without civil government, and without constitutions or other forms by virtue of which political relations could legally exist between them and the Federal Government.

2. "That Congress cannot be expected to recognize as valid the election of representatives from disorganized communities, which, from the very nature of the case, were unable to present their claim to representation under those established and recognized rules, the observance of which has been hitherto required.

3. "That Congress would not be justified in admitting such communities to a participation in the government of the country without first providing such constitutional or other guaranties as will tend to secure the civil rights of all citizens of the Republic ; a just eqality of representation ; protection against claims founded in rebellion and crime ; a temporary restoration of the right of suffrage to those who have not actively participated in the efforts to destroy the Union and overthrow the government ; and the exclusion from positions of public trust of at least a portion of those whose crimes have proved them to be enemies to the Union, and unworthy of public confidence."

In addition, the report contained an enumerated statement of "general facts and principles" which it was claimed were "applicable to all the States recently in rebellion." In this statement it was asserted that from the time war was declared the great majority of the Southerners "became and were in-surgents, rebels, traitors; and all of them assumed the political, legal, and practical relation of enemies of the United States." The States did not desist from war till "every vestige of State and Confederate government" was obliterated, "their people reduced to the condition of enemies conquered in war, entitled only by public law to such rights, privileges and conditions as might be vouch-safed by the conqueror." They thus had " no right to com-plain of temporary exclusion from Congress," until they could "show that they are qualified to resume federal relations. * * * They must prove that they have established, *with the consent of the people*, republican forms of government in har-mony with the Constitution and laws of the United States, that all hostile purposes have ceased, and should give adequate guaranties against future treason and rebellion—guaranties which shall prove satisfactory to the Government against which they rebelled, and by whose arms they were subdued." The rebels "were conquered by the people of the United States acting through all the co-ordinate branches of the Government, and not by the Executive alone. * * * The authority to restore rebels to political power in the Federal Government can be exercised only with the concurrence of all the departments in which political power is vested," and the proclamations of the President could only be regarded as provisional permission " to do certain acts, the effect and validity whereof is to be determined by the constitutional government, and not solely by the executive power." If the President had the power to "qualify persons to appoint Senators and elect Representatives, and empower others to appoint and elect them, he thereby practically controls the organization of the legislative department and destroys the constitutional form of government." [1]

[1] *House Reports*, No. 30, 39th Congress, 1st Session. McPherson, *History of Reconstruction*, pp. 84–93.

The report of the dissenting members of the committee, Messrs. Johnson, Rogers and Grider, was an ably prepared document embodying at length the doctrines of the minority in Congress, composed of the Democrats and the few Republicans who still sustained the President. As a matter of course the argument was built upon the premise that the so-called Confederate States were never legally separated from the Union, but were bound by all the obligations and entitled to all the privileges of other States. " In its nature the government is formed of and by States possessing equal rights and powers." A State cannot be held to have forfeited its rights. "To concede that by the illegal conduct of her own citizens she can be withdrawn from the Union, is virtually to concede the right of secession."

Were the States out of the Union, the minority continued, the submission to them of the proposed constitutional amendment would be absurd ; and such submission virtually conceded that the condition of the States remained unchanged. The constitutional power to suppress insurrection is for the preservation, not the subjugation of the State. " The continuance of the Union of all the States is necessary to the intended existence of the Government," and a different principle leads to disintegration. The war power, as such, cannot be used to extinguish the States ; the Government only seeks to suppress the insurrection, achieving which all the States resume their normal relations. The States now have organized governments, republican in form, and the manner in which they were formed is no concern of Congress. " Congress may admit new States, but a State once admitted ceases to be within its control and can never again be brought within it." There is nothing in the political condition of these States justifying their exclusion from representation in Congress. The proposed amendment would degrade the Southern States, as it would compel them to accept either a lessened representation or negro suffrage. Further, it interfered with the right of every State to regulate the franchise; and, by joining several subjects and requiring them to be voted on as a whole, deprived the people of the opportunity of passing on this important question separately.

8. The Joint Committee on Reconstruction had already reported two bills and one joint resolution which in its report of June 18 were declared to be the fruit of its labors. These were introduced in the House by Mr. Stevens, April 30. The resolution proposed an amendment to the Constitution, which, as finally amended, became the 14th Amendment.[1] The two accompanying bills were entitled respectively: (1) "A Bill to provide for restoring the States lately in insurrection to their full political rights." (2) "A Bill declaring certain persons ineligible to office under the Government of the United States."

The first of these bills prescribed the conditions on which a State lately in insurrection might secure representation in Congress, as well as a ten years' postponement of the exaction of any unpaid part of the direct tax of 1861. It provided that representation might be secured after the proposed amendment should have become a part of the Constitution, and the State seeking representation should have ratified such amendment. Postponement of the tax might be secured by ratifying the amendment. This bill served as a basis for general discussion of the best method of restoring to the States their political rights; but, no action was taken on it during this session, and it went over as unfinished business to the following December.

The second bill declared as ineligible to office: the President, Vice-President, and foreign agents of the Confederate States; "heads of departments of the United States, officers

___

[1] Gillet, *Democracy in the United States*, pp. 318–20.

of the army and navy of the United States, and all persons educated at the Military or Naval Academy of the United States," federal judges and members of the 36th Congress, who had given aid or comfort to the rebellion; Confederate officers above the rank of colonel in the army or master in the navy; governors of the Confederate States, and "those who have treated officers or soldiers or sailors of the army or navy of the United States, captured during the late war, otherwise than lawfully as prisoners of war." This bill was less fortunate than the first, since it failed even to receive consideration during the session.

The proposed constitutional amendment, however, fared better. It had been well demonstrated by the discussions during the session that an amendment to the Constitution would be submitted to the States, if a resolution could be framed which would satisfy the heterogeneous elements of the reconstruction party. But the framing of such a resolution had proved a very difficult matter. Stevens, and those most influenced by him, were especially radical in their doctrines, not hesitating to express their desire for the confiscation of rebels' property and for other extreme measures. Some believed that there should be nothing short of complete disfranchisement, for a term of years, of all who had aided the rebellion in any way—they had acted deliberately, and they must suffer the consequences. Others cared only for the disfranchisement of the more prominent offenders, and for the establishment of negro suffrage. Still another faction wished liberal terms to be offered to the States—limitations, but no interference.

The radicals recognized that their extreme ideas could not obtain congressional sanction, and made no effort to embody them in the plans submitted. From the beginning of the session various propositions were under discussion. Among these, the most attention was attracted by the various propositions to modify the existing basis of apportionment of representatives in Congress. Emancipation had rendered this necessary. The "three-fifths clause" of the Constitution having become inoperative, the increased representation resulting from the freeing of the slaves necessitated a change. The first plan was "to apportion Representatives according to the number of voters in the several States." [1] It was then proposed to exclude from the basis of representation all whose political rights were denied or abridged by any State on account of race or color. This plan, supported by Blaine and Conkling,[2] passed the House on January 31, 1866,[3] but was defeated in the Senate. Many felt that the measure was too stringent. The object was virtually to force upon the Southern States the enfranchisement of the negro.[4]

The Committee on Reconstruction hesitated for over a month after the defeat of this resolution in the Senate. It was finally decided that the only way in which the submission of the desired amendment could be effected, was to concede something to the conservative element of the Senate. Accordingly the draft of April 30 was presented as the recommendation of the committee. This passed the House without difficulty,[5] but encountered fierce opposition in the Senate. The House resolution contained a provision which would have summarily and unconditionally excluded from the franchise all participating in the rebellion, until July 4,

---

[1] *Congressional Globe*, 1st Session, 39th Congress, pp. 9, 10, 351.

[2] *Ibid.*, 141-2, 232. For general discussions and summaries of the debates on the 14th Amendment, see Wilson, *Rise and Fall of the Slave Power in America*, iii, 647–660; Wilson, *History of Reconstruction*, 218–266; Blaine, *Twenty Years of Congress*, ii, 193–214.

[3] The vote was: yeas, 120; nays, 46.

[4] *Congressional Globe*, 39th Congress, 1st Session, p. 2459.

[5] Yeas, 128, nays, 37.

1870. This was virtually a complete disfranchisement of the Southern people, and although only temporary, it was felt to be contrary to the spirit of our institutions and too indiscriminate a punishment. It was accordingly stricken out by a unanimous vote.[1] In its place Senator Howard proposed a clause which forms section 3 of the 14th Amendment as it now stands. This clause, while it withheld certain privileges of citizenship from participants in the rebellion who had previously held civil or military office and had taken an oath to support the Constitution of the United States, did not affect the vast majority of Southerners; and it provided that Congress might, by a two-thirds vote of each house, remove the disability of those who were excepted from the restoration of privileges. Moreover, in place of the plan supported by Blaine and Conkling for reducing the basis of representation, the Committee on Reconstruction presented a proposition which better satisfied the conservative element, and which stands to-day as section 2 of the 14th Amendment. It provided that in case the right of any male inhabitant of a State to vote was denied or abridged for any reason "except for participation in rebellion or other crime, the basis of representation therein shall be reduced in the proportion which the number of such male citizens shall bear to the whole number of male citizens twenty-one years of age in such state." It was argued that in this way fairness was assured, as a State could have no right to claim representation for that portion of her population which was denied the franchise.

On June 8, 1866, the final touches were put on the resolution. Five days later the House concurred in the Senate's revision, and the 14th Amendment was ready for the ratification of the States.

Johnson's followers and the Democrats bitterly opposed

[1] On May 29, *Congressional Globe*, 39th Congress, 1st Session, p. 2869.

the submission of this amendment. The more extreme of them asserted that the Republican majority acted from purely partisan motives. Fearful for the continuance of its supremacy, it desired to place before the States a measure so distasteful to the South as to ensure its rejection. In that way there would be an excuse for additional legislation to prevent the States from obtaining representation, and to preserve Republican control.[1] The composite character of the amendment provoked severe criticism. It was claimed that the sections should be submitted to the States as separate articles, to give opportunity for the rejection of some and the ratification of others. Senator Doolittle moved an amendment to this effect,[2] but the solid reconstruction majority could not be shaken, and the five sections were submitted to the States to stand or fall together. Technical objections were deemed unworthy of consideration when it was supposed to be necessary for the safety of the Union that all the sections should be ratified.

The inadvisability of submitting a constitutional amendment while eleven of the States were not permitted a voice in legislation was strongly urged by the opposition. The President reiterated the protest in his message of June 22, affirming that the submission of the proposed amendment to the States through the executive department was a purely ministerial duty, in no way committing the department to an approval of the action. The first section of the amendment was condemned as a subtle plan eventually to force negro suffrage upon the people as an incident of negro citizenship. It was claimed that the second discriminated too severely against the Southern States with their large preponderance of colored population, and that the third virtually forced them to insult their most respected citizens—a humilia-

---

[1] See Pollard's *Lost Cause Regained*, p. 74.

[2] *Senate Journal*, 39th Congress, 1st Session, p. 502.

tion which would drive them to renewed insurrection. The validity of some of the objections was proved by subsequent history; some have proved groundless; others still remain among the unsettled questions.

The reconstruction legislation of the first session of the 39th Congress closed with the restoration of Tennessee to the Union. Other measures were under consideration, but were not acted upon until the following session. The attitude of Tennessee, since her re-organization under the provisions of the proclamation of 1863, had been the most consistent of any of the Southern States.[1] From March 3, 1862, until March 3, 1865, Johnson, as military governor, had preserved law and order to a great extent. The formal reorganization of the State was undertaken by a convention of the loyal citizens convened January 8, 1865, acting upon the recommendation and personal approval of Johnson. This convention proposed the amendments to the constitution of the State, made necessary by the changes brought about by the war, and they were adopted by the loyal voters of the State on February 22. On March 4 a governor and legislature were elected, who assumed their duties on April 3. The work of the legislature was characterized by an apparent eagerness to do all that should be done by a State loyal to the Union.

The popular ratification of the amendments to the Constitution distinguished the action of Tennessee from that of the other Southern States, and this fact, united to her uniformly consistent attitude, formed the ground for the recommendation of the Committee on Reconstruction that this State should be restored to her former rights and privileges. This recommendation, in the form of a joint resolution, was reported from the committee by Mr. Bingham on March

---

[1] On the reorganization of Tennessee, see Blaine, *Twenty Years of Congress*, ii, 50–52, 214–17; Cox, *Three Decades of Federal Legislation*.

5,[1] but no action was taken until July 20. Tennessee's prompt action in ratifying the 14th Amendment[2] was taken as good evidence that her government was thoroughly reconstructed, and the State entitled to representation. Accordingly a substitute resolution, noting these facts, was introduced and passed, the Senate amending and passing it three days later. This declared Tennessee to be restored to her former relations to the Union, and entitled to representation in Congress,[3] but the preamble was used as a vehicle for the assertion of the sole power of Congress to restore State governments. President Johnson, while approving the resolution, explained in his message that his approval was " not to be construed as an acknowledgment of the right of Congress to pass laws preliminary to the admission of duly qualified representatives from any of the States," nor as committing him " to all the statements made in the preamble."

The session had proved far from fruitless, although nothing but the preliminary steps had been taken. The Freedmen's Bureau and civil rights bills constituted a temporary protection to the freedmen; the right of *habeas corpus* still remained suspended and military authority prevailed throughout the conquered region. The 14th Amendment was before the people, to be a rallying point for the autumn campaign. The lines between the presidential and congressional parties were now closely drawn. Each knew the strong and the weak points of its opponent. The issue must now be turned over to the people as final judges of its merits. The congressional elections of the fall would decide the issue, and also the future method of reconstruction.

[1] *House Reports*, No. 30, pt. 1; McPherson, *History of the Reconstruction*, pp. 105–6.

[2] Ratified by the Senate July 11, yeas, 15, nays, 6; by the House July 12, yeas, 43, nays, 11. Tennessee was the third State to ratify the amendment, Connecticut and New Hampshire being the first two.

[3] McPherson, *History of the Reconstruction*, pp. 151–4.

CHAPTER IV.

1. The four months following the adjournment of the first session of the 39th Congress were full of excitement. The public was thoroughly aroused, and all incidents were considered in the light they threw upon the question of the hour. The President's uncompromising hostility to the 14th Amendment brought about a crisis in the Cabinet.[1] William Dennison, Postmaster-General, was the first to declare the impossibility of maintaining cabinet relations with the President. He resigned on July 11, and A. W. Randall, of Wisconsin, First Assistant Postmaster-General, was appointed in his place. Mr. Randall was a devoted adherent of the administration, and president of the National Union Club which called the convention of August 14. The second resignation was that of James Speed, Attorney-General, on July 18. Coming from Kentucky, Mr. Speed had had the reputation of being quite conservative in his views regarding reconstruction, and his formal notice of separation from the President created no little excitement. His intimate connection with the administration gave unusual force to his denunciation of its policy, made at the time of taking the chair as permanent president of the convention of Southern loyalists. Henry Stanbery of Ohio was appointed as his successor, and retained his position until he resigned to assist in the defense of the President in the impeachment trial. A few days after Mr. Speed's withdrawal, the Secretary of the

[1] Blaine, *Twenty Years of Congress*, ii, 219–220.

Interior, James Harlan, tendered his resignation, and O. H. Browning, of Illinois, was appointed to fill the vacancy.

It is altogether probable that these resignations would have been made earlier than they were, had it not been feared that the control of these important administrative departments would fall into the hands of those who would use their powers in opposition to Congress. But the time had come when the incumbents considered that by the retention of the offices they were being forced to share the odium attached to the President, and deemed total separation from him as the best method of justification.

The laws discriminating against the colored man, and the numerous instances of cruelty which had been reported to the North, were an important factor in creating and sustaining the common feeling of hostility to the administration. But the New Orleans riots, occurring on July 30, did more to rouse the people of the North, and convince them that stern measures were necessary, than all that had preceded. The massacre stood out vividly against the background of " black laws," and furnished an argument of the most effective kind to be used in the campaign.

2. The riots were of a peculiarly exasperating character. The constitutional convention of 1864, summoned by the proclamation of Major General Banks, had passed resolutions giving the president of the convention power " to reconvoke the convention for any cause." A majority of the members came to the conclusion, in the spring of 1866, that the State constitution should be amended, to place it in harmony with the congressional policy.[1] They determined to have the convention reconvoked for this purpose. The president,

---

[1] The Congressional committee of investigation, appointed at the beginning of the 2d session, in December, submitted a detailed report of the riots. See *House Reports*, No. 16, 2d Session, 39th Congress. See also Blaine, *Twenty Years of Congress*, ii, 233–237.

Judge E. H. Durell, declined to take advantage of his pre-
rogative, but the delegates, not to be thwarted in this way,
proceeded to elect a president *pro tem.* who was willing to
issue the desired proclamation. The governor of the State,
J. M. Wells, concurred in this rather questionable procedure,
and issued a proclamation for an election to fill existing
vacancies.

It being well understood that negro suffrage was one of
the ultimate objects desired by the supporters of the proposed constitutional convention, active hostility to the
movement rapidly developed. The proclamation of the
president *pro tem.* called for the assembling of the delegates
on July 30; and though the only object of this meeting was
to determine officially the existing vacancies to be filled in
the fall elections, the enemies to the enfranchisement of the
freedmen determined to crush the movement in its incipient
stage. It is an easy matter to stir up the passions and
prejudices of the people, and the indiscreet speeches of
certain of the delegates only added to the popular excitement. A negro procession organized in honor of the convention was attacked by a mob in front of Mechanics' Hall,
where the convention was in session. The attack was soon
extended to the hall itself, the police of the city joining
hands with the assailants. When the riot was over nearly
two hundred persons were found to have been killed or
wounded, the greatest sufferers being the negroes, who were
shot down in front of the hall without mercy.

The flagrancy of the act, the connivance of the city authorities, and the fact that, while legal steps were taken against
the delegates and innocent spectators, the actual murderers
were in no way molested, furnished to the people of the incensed North ample proof of the inability of the South to
maintain local government, and of the advisability of refusing
to restore these States to their former position in the Union.

New Orleans was taken as a fair example of what might happen at any place in the South. There was no satisfactory justification for these acts of violence, and there was little inclination in the North to consider the legal technicalities involved in the attempt to amend the constitution of Louisiana. They simply took cognizance of the fact that about fifty loyal citizens had been murdered in cold blood, with the city authorities silently acquiescing. In the face of such a fact, the solicitude of the President to preserve the "inherent rights of the States" did not appeal to the masses, and Johnson was forced to begin his campaign badly handicapped.

But, in addition to the blow given to the theory of the administration, Johnson was forced to labor against a certain amount of personal censure, brought about by his supposed attitude before the riots and his known attitude after them. It was freely charged that he was in full sympathy with the determination of the Mayor of New Orleans, and the Lieutenant-Governor and Attorney-General of Louisiana, to prevent the convention from accomplishing its plans. In support of the charge, his answer to the inquiry as to whether the military power would interfere with the attempt to arrest the members of the convention upon criminal process was cited. His reply was as follows:[1] "The military will be expected to sustain, and not to obstruct or interfere with the proceedings of the court." While this may have indicated too great confidence in the civil authorities of Louisiana, it certainly did not imply any connivance in or sympathy with the summary proceeding of July 30. Possibly the well-known opposition of Johnson to negro suffrage may have stimulated the rioters to bolder defiance of Northern sentiment, but censure of him can extend

---

[1] *House Reports*, No. 16, 39th Congress, 2d Session, p. 26.

no farther. But, in his political canvass in the fall,[1] while endeavoring in every way to discredit the 39th Congress in the eyes of the people, he committed a grave error by an indirect defense of the rioters, attacking the members of the convention as traitors who incited the negro population to rioting, and throwing the responsibility of the whole affair back upon Congress as having originated and fostered the plan to force negro suffrage upon Louisiana.[2]

3. The fall campaign was formally opened by the supporters of the presidential policy, who had immediately accepted the report of the Committee on Reconstruction as the platform of the Republican anti-administration faction, and had determined to appeal on that issue to the people. Their hope was that the conservative element of the population, thoroughly worn out by the struggle, would uphold the speedy restoration of the Southern States, and that thereby a coalition might be made between the Democrats and the administration Republicans strong enough to unseat many of the radical members, reverse the majority, and so give the administration control in the 40th Congress.

The first steps were promptly taken. The executive committee of the National Union Club, a political organization established in Washington by supporters of the administration, issued on June 25, just one week after the submission of the report of the Committee on Reconstruction, a call for a national convention to be held in Philadelphia on August 14.[3] Delegates to this convention were to be chosen by those supporting the administration and agreeing to certain " fundamental propositions " which formed the plat-

---

[1] See below for an account of this canvass.

[2] *House Reports*, No. 16, 39th Congress, 2d Session, pp. 24–27; McPherson, *History of the Reconstruction*, 137.

[3] McPherson, *History of the Reconstruction*, 118, 119; Blaine, *Twenty Years of Congress*, ii, 220–223.

form of the conservatives. These propositions maintained the absolute indissolubility of the Union, the universal supremacy of the Constitution and acts of Congress in pursuance thereof, the constitutional guarantee to maintain the rights, dignity and equality of the States, and the right of each State to prescribe the qualifications of electors, without any federal interference. They declared that the usurpation and centralization of powers infringing upon the rights of the States " would be a revolution, dangerous to republican government, and destructive of liberty;" that the exclusion of loyal senators and representatives, properly chosen and qualified under the Constitution and laws, was unjust and revolutionary; that as the war was at an end, " war measures should also cease, and should be followed by measures of peaceful administration;" and that the restoration of the rights and privileges of the States was necessary for the prosperity of the Union. This formal call was approved, and its principles endorsed by the Democratic congressmen, who issued an address to the " People of the United States " on July 4, urging them to act promptly in the selection of delegates to the convention.

In accordance with the call, every State and Territory was represented in the convention. A glance at the list of delegates shows that they included many of the prominent Democrats of the country, re-enforced by a number of the prominent Republicans [1] who were in sympathy with the administration. The enthusiastic manner in which the summons was answered seemed to the friends of the administration to indicate an unquestionable overthrow of the radicals. They thought that harmony was soon to reign over all portions of the Union, which was once more being drawn closely together by the watchword " National Union."

---

[1] Among these Republicans were Thurlow Weed, Edgar Cowan, James R. Doolittle, A. W. Randall, O. H. Browning, James Dixon, Henry J. Raymond, R. S. Hale, J. A. Dix, Marshall O. Roberts and Montgomery Blair.

Reverdy Johnson, who had submitted in the Senate the minority report of the Committee on Reconstruction, was chosen chairman, and Senator Cowan, of Pennsylvania, chairman of the committee on resolutions. The resolutions were reported on August 17, and unanimously adopted by the convention. They re-affirmed the fundamental principles set forth in the call of June 25, and appealed to the people of the United States to elect none to Congress but those who "will receive to seats therein loyal representatives from every State in allegiance to the United States." They reiterated the claim that in the ratification of constitutional amendments all the States " have an equal and an indefeasible right to a voice and vote thereon." In concession to Northern sentiment, they declared that the South had no desire to re-establish slavery ; that the civil rights of the freedmen were to be respected, the rebel debt repudiated, the national debt declared sacred and inviolable, and the duty of the government to recognize the services of the federal soldiers and sailors admitted. A final resolution commended the President in the highest terms, as worthy of the nation, "having faith unassailable in the people and in the principles of free government." [1]

These views were fully elaborated in an address prepared by Henry J. Raymond, and read before the convention. Little attempt was made to qualify or render less offensive the argument that the Southern States must be allowed their representation in Congress, whether or not such action was for the best interest of the Union. Referring to this the address declared that "we have no right, for such reasons, to deny to any portion of the States or people rights expressly conferred upon them by the Constitution of the United States." We should trust to the ability of our people

[1] McPherson, *History of the Reconstruction*, 240–1.

"to protect and defend, under all contingencies and by whatever means may be required, its honor and welfare."[1]

A committee of the convention hastened formally to present its proceedings to President Johnson, who had taken the keenest interest in the plans of the National Union party. In his remarks to the committee he feelingly referred to the somewhat theatrical entrance of the delegates of South Carolina and Massachusetts, "arm in arm, marching into that vast assemblage, and thus giving evidence that the two extremes had come together again, and that for the future they were united, as they had been in the past, for the preservation of the Union." Speaking to a sympathetic audience, who applauded him to the echo, and believing that the people were now endorsing his opposition to Congress, he saw no necessity for tempering his statements, and cast aside his discretion. His characterization of Congress was as follows: "We have witnessed, in one department of the government, every endeavor to prevent the restoration of peace, harmony and union. We have seen hanging upon the verge of the Government, as it were, a body called, or which assumes to be, the Congress of the United States, while in fact it is a Congress of only a part of the States. We have seen this Congress pretend to be for the Union, when its every step and act tended to perpetuate disunion and make a disruption of the States inevitable. Instead of promoting reconciliation and harmony, its legislation has partaken of the character of penalties, retaliation and revenge. This has been the course and policy of one portion of the Government."[2] Again, to show the disinterestedness of his own course, he said: "If I had wanted authority, or if I had wished to perpetuate my own power, how easily could I have held and wielded that power which

[1] Blaine, *Twenty Years of Congress*, ii, 222.

[2] McPherson, *History of the Reconstruction*, 127.

was placed in my hands by the measure called the Freedmen's Bureau bill (laughter and applause). With an army,
which it placed at my discretion, I could have remained at
the capital of the nation, and with fifty or sixty millions of
appropriations at my disposal, with the machinery to be un-
locked by my own hands, with my satraps and dependents
in every town and village, with the Civil Rights bill following as an auxiliary (laughter), and with the patronage and
other appliances of the Government, I could have proclaimed
myself dictator." ("That's true!" and applause.)[1]

But his indiscretions did not end with speeches before his
sympathizers. Two weeks later he started on a trip,
nominally to assist in the ceremony of laying the corner-
stone of the Douglas monument in Chicago.[2] As a matter
of fact, however, he was merely taking advantage of an opportunity to defend his policy publicly. Johnson was of
too impassioned a nature to be able to judge as to how far
the President of the United States could afford to adopt the
methods of the stump speaker. All constraint was thrown
away, and he acted at many times the part most natural to
him, that of a popular orator addressing the masses. His
speeches at no time lacked clearness. All could see where
he stood, and nothing was left for speculation.

His first important effort while on his journey was at New
York on August 29, where he responded to a toast proposed
by the mayor of the city. In this speech he defined the issue
as follows: "The rebellion has been suppressed, and in the
suppression of the rebellion it [the government] has * * *
established the great fact that these States have not the
power, and it denied their right, by forcible or peaceable

---

[1] McPherson, *History of the Reconstruction*, 129. This manner of indicating his
disinterestedness caused great offense in some quarters. See the account below
of the Pittsburg convention of soldiers and sailors of September 26.

[2] See Blaine, *Twenty Years of Congress*, ii, 237–239.

means, to separate themselves from the Union. (Cheers, "Good!") That having been determined and settled by the Government of the United States in the field and in one of the departments of the government—the executive department of the government—there is an open issue; there is another department of your government which has declared by its official acts, and by the position of the Government, notwithstanding the rebellion was suppressed for the purpose of preserving the Union of the States and establishing the doctrine that the States could not secede, yet they have practically assumed and declared and carried up to the present point, that the Government was dissolved and the States were out of the Union. (Cheers.) We who contended for the opposite doctrine years ago contended that even the States had not the right to peaceably secede; and one of the means and modes of possible secession was that the States of the Union might withdraw their representatives from the Congress of the United States, and that would be practical dissolution. We denied that they had any such right. (Cheers.) And now, when the doctrine is established that they have no right to withdraw, and the rebellion is at an end * * * we find that in violation of the Constitution, in express terms as well as in spirit, that these States of the Union have been and still are denied their representation in the Senate and in the House of Representatives." [1] Then, speaking of the people of the South: "* * Do we want to humiliate them and degrade them and drag them in the dust? ('No, no!' Cheers.) I say this, and I repeat it here to-night, I do not want them to come back to this Union a degraded and debased people. (Loud cheers.) They are not fit to be a part of this great American family if they are degraded and treated with ignominy and contempt. I want them when they come

[1] McPherson, *History of the Reconstruction*, 130.

back to become a part of this great country, an honored portion of the American people."[1]

Another representative speech was the one which he made in Cleveland on September 3: "I tell you, my countrymen, I have been fighting the South, and they have been whipped and crushed, and they acknowledge their defeat and accept the terms of the Constitution; and now, as I go around the circle, having fought traitors at the South, I am prepared to fight traitors at the North. (Cheers.) God willing, with your help we will do it. (Cries of 'We won't.') It will be crushed North and South, and this glorious Union of ours will be preserved. (Cheers.) I do not come here as the Chief Magistrate of twenty-five States out of thirty-six. (Cheers.) I came here to-night with the flag of my country and the Constitution of thirty-six States untarnished. Are you for dividing this country? (Cries of 'No.') Then I am President, and I am President of the whole United States. (Cheers.)"[2]

Speeches of this nature, coming at a time when the out-

---

[1] McPherson, *History of the Reconstruction*, 131, 132.

[2] McPherson, 135. The following is a good example of the manner in which Johnson lowered himself to the level of the disorderly element, who made a bedlam out of some of the meetings he attended. The extract is from the Cleveland speech: "Who can come and place his finger on one pledge I ever violated, or one principle I ever proved false to? (A voice, 'How about New Orleans?' Another voice, 'Hang Jeff Davis.') Hang Jeff Davis, he says. (Cries of 'No' and 'Down with him!') Hang Jeff Davis, he says. (A voice, 'Hang Thad. Stevens and Wendell Phillips.') Hang Jeff Davis. Why don't you hang him? (Cries of 'Give us the opportunity.') Have you not got the court? Have not you got the Attorney General? (A voice, 'Who is your Chief Justice who has refused to sit upon the trial?' Cheers.) I am not the Chief Justice. I am not the prosecuting attorney. (Cheers.) I am not the jury.

"I will tell you what I did do. I called upon your Congress that is trying to break up the government. (Cries, 'You be d—d !' and cheers mingled with hisses. Great confusion. 'Don't get mad, Andy.') Well, I will tell you who is mad. 'Whom the gods wish to destroy, they first make mad.' Did your Congress order them to be tried? ('Three cheers for Congress ')," etc.

rages in the South had so greatly incensed the North, had a
most depressing influence upon the fortunes of the National
Union party, and failed utterly in the object for which they
were intended.   The trip proved to be a grave political mistake.   The undignified spectacle of a President receiving
coarse personal abuse and retorting in scarcely less coarse expressions was quickly taken advantage of by his opponents;
and the phrase " swinging around the circle" has assumed
historic dignity as a description of his journey.

4. The " off year " national convention plan adopted by
the National Union Club was immediately accepted by the
congressional party, which was no less active in preparations
for the struggle.   On July 4, the same day on which the
Democratic congressmen issued their address to the people,
representative Southern Unionists,[1] supporters of Congress,
issued a call to " the Loyal Unionists of the South," for a
convention to be held in Philadelphia on September 3.[2]
The call stated that the convention was "for the purpose of
bringing the loyal Unionists of the South " into conjunction
with the true friends of republican government in the North.
* * The time has come when the restructure of Southern
State government must be laid on constitutional principles.
* * * We maintain that no State, either by its organic law
or legislation, can make transgression on the rights of the
citizen legitimate.   * * *   Under the doctrine of ' State
sovereignty,' with rebels in the foreground, controlling
Southern legislatures, and embittered by disappointment in
their schemes to destroy the Union, there will be no safety
for the loyal element of the South.   Our reliance for protection is now on Congress, and the great Union party that has
stood and is standing by our nationality, by the constitu-

---

[1] Tennessee, Texas, Georgia, Missouri, Virginia, North Carolina and Alabama
were represented among the signers to the call.

[2] McPherson, *History of the Reconstruction*, 124.

tional rights of the citizen, and by the beneficent principles of the government."

The convention met at the time appointed, with representatives present from all the lately insurrectionary States.[1] James Speed of Kentucky, Attorney-General until July 18, was elected permanent chairman. For purposes of co-operation, the Northern States had been invited to send delegations, and all responded. Thus the convention was as truly national as the " National Union " convention of August 14 had been. It was decided, however, that for the purpose of rendering the declaration of the Southern Unionists more significant, the Northern and Southern Unionists should hold their sessions separately, and Governor Curtin of Pennsylvania was accordingly elected chairman of the Northern section.

The resolutions of the Southern section were reported by Governor Hamilton of Texas, chairman of the committee on resolutions, and they naturally endorsed the action of Congress in its entirety.[2] While demanding the restoration of the States, they declared Johnson's policy to be " unjust, oppressive, and intolerable," and that restoration under his " inadequate conditions " would only magnify " the perils and sorrows of our condition." They agreed to support Congress and to endeavor to secure the ratification of the 14th Amendment. Congress alone had power to determine the political status of the States and the rights of the people, " to the exclusion of the independent action of any and every other department of the Government." " The organizations of the unrepresented States, assuming to be state governments, not having been legally established," were declared " not legitimate governments until reorganized by Congress." In addition to these resolutions, an address " from the loyal

[1] Blaine, *Twenty Years of Congress*, ii, 224–228.
[2] McPherson, *History of the Reconstruction*, 241, 242.

men of the South to their fellow-citizens of the United States,"
was prepared and adopted after the formal adjournment of
the convention.[1] This reaffirmed, in far stronger terms, the
condemnation of President Johnson, specifying many ways in
which he had wrought injury to them, and closing with the
following significant and powerful declaration: " We affirm
that the loyalists of the South look to Congress with affection-
ate gratitude and confidence, as the only means to save us from
persecution, exile and death itself; and we also declare that
there can be no security for us or our children, there can
be no safety for the country against the fell spirit of slavery,
now organized in the form of serfdom, unless the Government, by national and appropriate legislation, enforced by
national authority, shall confer on every citizen in the States
we represent the American birthright of impartial suffrage
and equality before the law. This is the one all-sufficient
remedy. This is our great need and pressing necessity."[2]

A third convention of the year was the Cleveland convention of soldiers and sailors,[3] organized on September 17,
with General Wood of the regular army as chairman.
This convention was composed of supporters of the administration, and, like the National Union convention, contained a considerable proportion of Democrats. The resolutions endorsed those of the National Union convention,
and declared that " our object in taking up arms to suppress
the late rebellion was to defend and maintain the supremacy
of the Constitution, and to preserve the Union with all the
dignity, equality, and rights of the States unimpaired."

The great mass of the soldiers, however, were earnest sup-

---

[1] McPherson, *History of the Reconstruction*, 242.

[2] The address was prepared by Senator Creswell, of Maryland. See Blaine,
Twenty Years of Congress, ii, 223–228.

[3] McPherson, *History of the Reconstruction*, 243; Blaine, *Twenty Years of
Congress*, ii, 228-230.

porters of Congress, and the results of the Cleveland convention were disappointing to its originators; its principal effect was to create great enthusiasm over the anti-administration convention of soldiers and sailors, which met in Pittsburg on September 25 and 26.[1] This demonstration was intended to offset whatever influence the Cleveland convention might have had over the people, and it proved wonderfully effective. It was estimated that at least twenty-five thousand old soldiers were in the city at the time. The cause for this enthusiastic support is not difficult to find. The policy of the administration appealed to the moderates—those who wished as rapid a restoration to former conditions as possible, and those who were most influenced by the appeal to so-called justice. The majority of the soldiers, on the contrary, those who had made the greatest sacrifices for their country, were the most sensitive concerning the results of their sacrifices. Thoroughly accustomed to the thought of their great accomplishments, the manumission of the slaves and the preservation of the integrity of national power, they were keen to resent any steps which they thought tended toward the annulling of these results. With this natural bias, the arguments which the congressional party brought to bear upon them were accepted with enthusiasm; and many of the leaders went into the political campaign to be followed by the same soldiers who had followed them through their military campaigns. The convention, however, was in no sense a convention of officers. While the permanent president, Jacob D. Cox, of Ohio,[2] had been a general of volunteers, the temporary chairman, L. E. Dudley, had been a private, and the majority of the offices of the convention were filled by men below the rank of lieutenant.

[1] Blaine, *Twenty Years of Congress*, ii, 230–233.

[2] General John A. Logan was first chosen president, but was unable to attend.

As was to be expected from the nature of the convention, the feeling against the administration was stronger and declared in more impassioned tones than in the previous anti-administration convention. Its influence upon the country was correspondingly greater. The army, recognized at this time as the great preserver of the commonwealth, had great influence over all classes of citizens. The anti-administration conventions, the New Orleans massacre, and the violent attacks on Congress by the President while "swinging around the circle," assured the triumph of the congressional party.

The resolutions adopted at Pittsburgh were presented by General Butler.[1] They were emphatic in tone, commencing with the declaration that "the action of the present Congress in passing the pending constitutional amendment is wise, prudent, and just," and that it was unfortunate that it was not received in the proper spirit, the terms being the mildest "ever granted to subdued rebels." The President's policy was declared to be "as dangerous as it is unwise," and "if consummated it would render the sacrifices of the nation useless." The power "to pass all acts of legislation that are necessary for the complete restoration of the Union" was declared to rest in Congress. The declaration of the President to the committee of the National Union convention, that he could have made himself dictator through the Freedmen's Bureau, aided by the army and navy, was characterized as an insult to "every soldier and sailor in the Republic." The obligation of the soldiers and sailors to the loyal men of the South was acknowledged; and it was added: "We will stand by and protect with our lives, if necessary, those brave men who remain true to us when all around are false and faithless."

This, the most successful of the four conventions, com-

[1] McPherson, *History of the Reconstruction*, 242, 243.

pleted the remarkable series of national gatherings organized for effect on the State elections. They were all character- ized by frankness of statement, and by clear recognition of the points at issue. But, as frequently happens in political campaigns, the most important incidents were those which were not designed to affect national issues. The riot at New Orleans was intended, by its participants, to affect only Louisiana politics, yet all the Southern States were com- pelled to share the responsibility. The same thing was true of all other incidents through which the South manifested, during these critical months, an unwillingness to accept the political results of the war.

5. The fall elections resulted in a decisive victory for the congressional policy, which secured a two-thirds majority in both houses. The protests of the President were shown to lack popular support, and his vetoes in the coming sessions were to be considered as merely one necessary step in the legislative formality of passing a bill. The country had decreed that Johnson could not have a voice in legislation. The campaign had been in all respects disastrous to the Presi- dent. The support which he had received was mainly drawn from the Democratic party, and was of a half-hearted nature; for, however nearly they agreed in theory, the fact still re- mained that he was nominally a Republican President, and that almost all of his patronage was bestowed upon Republicans. He had thrown out decided hints that he would reverse his policy. For example, in St. Louis, on September 8, he said: "I believe in the good old doctrine advocated by Washington, Jefferson and Madison—of rotation in office. These people who have been enjoying these offices seem to have lost sight of this doctrine. I believe that one set of men have enjoyed the emoluments of office long enough. They should let another portion of the people have a chance. * * * Congress says he [the President]

shall not turn them out, and they are trying to pass laws to prevent it being done.   Well, let me say to you, if you will stand by me in this action (cheers), if you will stand by me in trying to give the people a fair chance—soldiers and citizens—to participate in these offices, God being willing I will kick them out. * * * God willing, with your help, I will veto their measures whenever any of them come to me."[1] But all this failed to give him that which he prided himself so much on having, the support of the people; and, so far as reconstruction was concerned, his influence was ended by the fall elections of 1866.

6. While such was the general result of the campaign, the South voted to sustain the President's policy.   The fact that Johnson had taken direct issue with Congress, and was actively supporting Democratic principles, had a wonderful influence upon the South.   The papers enthusiastically prophesied the complete overthrow of the Republican party.   They reasoned that the enormous patronage of the President would ensure him a following so powerful that its coalition with Democracy could not but result in victory. Then, they reasoned, it would only be necessary to wait until the convening of the 40th Congress, when the obnoxious amendment would be discredited and the States readmitted to the possession of all their rights and privileges without further delay or conditions.   They utterly failed to realize the injury which their discriminative legislation, the New Orleans riots, the widely spread reports of cruelty and oppression, and the defiant attitude of their press, had inflicted on their cause.   They only saw that the administration and Congress were estranged, and believed that to be a sure indication of final success.

In this frame of mind they came to the polls, and in all the Southern States overwhelming Democratic majorities

[1] McPherson, *History of the Reconstruction*, 140.

evidenced the popular sentiment among the dominant classes. Accordingly, when the State legislatures convened, the 14th amendment was rejected almost unanimously in all except Tennessee, which had ratified it in July. Delaware, Maryland and Kentucky, the border Union States, also rejected the amendment, allying themselves with the Southern cause. Twenty-one of the remaining twenty-four States ratified the amendment, endorsing thereby the action of Congress.[1] Iowa, Nebraska and California did not act upon the amendment at this time.

Had Thaddeus Stevens and Charles Sumner been able to persuade Congress to adopt their theory of the status of the Southern States, the amendment would have been assumed to be a part of the Constitution, as twenty-one States were more than three-quarters of twenty-seven, the total number of States represented in Congress. But the majority of congressmen were never able to adopt, in its entirety, the theory that the rebellion had utterly destroyed the States and left them mere territory. It preferred to accomplish the same result by less violent means. The legislation enacted as a result of the attitude of the South towards the amendment practically treated the States as conquered territory, yet they were counted in determining the ratification of both the 13th and the 14th amendment.

The defiant attitude taken by the Southern legislatures was a grave mistake. The most of them did not convene until Congress was again in session, after the defeat of the administration, and when they should have been able to see that their only hope was in submission. But the South, ever too ready to act first and consider the consequences afterwards, only saw in the proposed amendment an insult to the white race and an injustice to their leaders. That they should be asked deliberately to inflict upon themselves

[1] McPherson, *History of the Reconstruction*, 194.

this punishment, seemed a humiliation which self-respect could permit them only to spurn. They did not stop to realize that the rejection of these terms would cause measures still more severe to be enacted.

CHAPTER V.

THE CONGRESSIONAL THEORY FULLY DEVELOPED.

1. The second session of the 39th Congress opened with its members in a far different frame of mind from that in which they had assembled in 1865. Then they had approached their work with hesitation; their plans were not formulated; they could not know how far the country would sustain them in their opposition to the President. Now, in the flush of victory, their policy sustained, the President discredited, with their two-thirds majority in both houses unbroken, they were prepared to proceed to enact legislation which not only should secure that which had been accomplished already, but also should settle finally the problem of reconstruction, and place the President in a position where he could do no harm.[1]

Much curiosity had been felt as to the attitude which Johnson would take in his annual message. He believed thoroughly in the righteousness of his cause, and had such implicit confidence in the unerring judgment of the people that he had deemed it impossible that his policy would be repudiated. The results of the election were a great disappointment to him, and some had believed that he would introduce into the message the abuse which he had so unsparingly inflicted upon Congress during the campaign. The message, however, contained nothing approaching virulence, but on the contrary was a document eminently

[1] Scott, *Reconstruction during the Civil War*, 290 ff.

creditable to the President.[1] It restated in a powerful way the constitutional position of the administration, and defended its actions in a dignified yet spirited manner. The fearlessness of his attitude was characteristic; the argumentative brilliancy of its presentation was unsurpassed. Unmindful of the fact that Congress had assembled to complete the overthrow of his policy of reconstruction, he reminded Congress that "the Constitution of the United States makes it the duty of the President to recommend to the consideration of Congress" such measures as he shall judge necessary or expedient. "* * * I know," he said, "of no measure more imperatively demanded by every consideration of national interest, sound policy, and equal justice, than the admission of loyal members from the now unrepresented States. * * * The interests of the nation are best to be promoted by the revival of fraternal relations, the complete obliteration of our past differences, and the re-inauguration of all pursuits of peace."[2] The message closed with the request: "Let us endeavor to preserve harmony between the co-ordinate departments of the Government, that each in its proper sphere may cordially co-operate with the other in securing the maintenance of the Constitution, the preservation of the Union, and the perpetuity of our free institutions."

Unfortunately for the country, there could be no harmony "between the co-ordinate departments of the Government," where there was such fundamental disagreement. Neither side proposed to retreat an inch from the stand taken, and the message served no other purpose than to leave a very excellent state paper as a memento of the session.

[1] *House Journal*, 2d Session, 39th Congress, 12–23; McPherson, *History of the Reconstruction*, 143–147.

[2] *House Journal*, 2d Session, 39th Congress, 15.

The Joint Committee on Reconstruction [1] was immediately re-appointed by a concurrent resolution. Only one change was necessary—Mr. Grider, of Kentucky, one of the minority members, had died during the recess of Congress, and in his place Mr. Hise, of the same State, was appointed. The committee immediately resumed its labors, and proceeded to frame a bill " for the more efficient government of the rebel States." The developments of the last three months had created a sentiment favorable to more stringent conditions of re-admission, and the action of the various Southern legislatures, who were rejecting the 14th amendment during this period, served as a further stimulus to vigorous action.

2. Several weeks elapsed before the committee was willing to adopt any definite plan. Finally, on February 4, 1867, Mr. Williams reported from the committee, a bill to the Senate; [2] it was referred back to the committee, and was formally reported to the House by Mr. Stevens on the 6th. [3]

The preamble to the bill declared that in the absence of legal State governments there was no adequate protection for person and property, and that therefore it was necessary to enforce peace and good order until loyal State governments could be established. To this end " the so-called States shall be divided into military districts," five in number, Virginia to constitute the first, North Carolina and South Carolina the second, Georgia, Alabama, and Florida the third, Mississippi and Arkansas the fourth, and Louisiana and Texas the fifth. The General of the Army was " to assign to the command of each of said districts an officer of the regular army not below the rank of brigadier-general, and to detail a suffi-

---

[1] The resolution passed the House on December 4, and the Senate on December 5. *House Journal*, 2d Session, 39th Congress, 30; *Senate Journal*, 2d Session, 39th Congress, 22.

[2] *Senate Journal*, 2d Session, 39th Congress, 202.

[3] *House Journal*, 2d Session, 39th Congress, 345.

cient force to enable such officer to enforce his authority."
The officer in command of a district was to have complete
authority to protect the civil rights of all, suppress insurrection and preserve order. To assist him he could employ
civil or military tribunals at his discretion, but no capital
punishment, imposed by a military tribunal, should be
executed without the approval of the officer in charge of the
district. Writs of *habeas corpus* should not be issued by
federal courts or judicial officers except on endorsement of
some commissioned officer in the district.

The discussion of the bill began on the day following its introduction. Mr. Stevens, with his usual impetuosity, wished
for an immediate vote. The bill seemed more moderate to
him than the South deserved, and with the large Republican
majority intent upon some such legislation, he could see no
reason for delay. The bill was clearly worded and all could
understand it perfectly. But there was an influential element that preferred to make haste slowly, and many hours
were given up to debate before the final passage of the bill
by the House, on February 20.

The measure certainly was exceedingly radical as it was
reported from the committee. As Mr. Le Blond, of Ohio,
said: "It strikes at the civil governments in those States.
It ignores State lines. It destroys their civil governments.
It breaks down the judicial system in those States."[1] The
distrust of the President was evidenced by empowering General Grant to appoint the commanders of the military districts, ignoring the President as commander-in-chief of the
army. Most important of all, the bill as it stood was the
action of a conquering power over conquered territory. It
provided for an indefinite military control over the territory,
and specified no mode in which a State might free herself

---

[1] *Congressional Globe*, 2d Session, 39th Congress, 1074.

from the onerous conditions. It was not a measure of reconstruction; it was a measure of subjugation.

Of course none of its supporters had the slightest idea of
its being more than a temporary measure, but even temporary measures must be considered in all their aspects. Their
idea was that expressed by Mr. Brandegee of Connecticut
when he said: "It holds those revolted communities in the
grasp of war until the rebellion shall have laid down its
spirit, as two years ago it formally laid down its arms.[1]

Mr. Bingham took an active part in the opposition to the
adoption of the bill as it stood. Representing the more
conservative branch of the anti administration party, he suggested on the opening day of the discussion amendments
which would make the bill more desirable. On February 12
he submitted an amendment, the essential features of which
were finally adopted, but which encountered the fiercest
opposition and was only carried when compromise between
the House and the Senate was found to be impossible. His
amendment provided as conditions for re-admitting a State
to representation in Congress: Ratification of the 14th
amendment; such modification of State constitution and
laws as would make them conform to that amendment; a
constitutional provision for negro suffrage; and the approval
of the constitution by Congress as republican in form and
consistent with the Constitution and laws of the United
States.

Mr. Blaine proposed an amendment similar in its aim to
that of Mr. Bingham, who accepted it as a substitute. But
the House was opposed to providing any loop-holes by
which the States could escape the provisions of the act.
The feeling that the South had been weighed in the balance
and found wanting, that its whole attitude was that of
defiance, and that it would endeavor to undo all that had

[1] *Congressional Globe*, 2d Session, 39th Congress, 1076.

been done as soon as it could obtain an opportunity, was sufficiently strong to defeat an attempt to refer the bill to the Judiciary Committee with instructions to incorporate the amendment. Instead, a substitute measure, introduced by Mr. Stevens, which differed but little from the original bill, passed the House on February 13.[1]

The great struggle now began in the Senate, where the Blaine amendment was moved by Mr. Johnson of Maryland, on February 15. There was an influential element which feared that its adoption would utterly nullify the object of the bill—to govern the States until they could be re-admitted with safety. Their objections were based on the same principles that had proved fatal to the amendment in the House. "I see," said Senator Howard, "in this amendment a fatal snare by which we shall be deceived in the end, by which we are to be deluded into a premature re-admission of the rebel States in such a manner as to make us ultimately repent of our folly and rashness. * * * It is a snare by which increased representation from the rebel States may come into Congress, * * while we have no security at all that the extended elective franchise will be continued in the rebel States to the black population. They can disfranchise them whenever they see fit after having secured increased representation."[2]

The Senate, more conservative than the House, could not muster such a strong opposition to the amendment. It was rejected, but rejected in order to open the way for another amendment in the form of a substitute bill, which was moved by Senator Sherman.[3] The substitute had been agreed upon in a Republican caucus, and was accordingly carried. Its first four sections contained nearly all the feat-

---

[1] *Congressional Globe*, 2d Session, 39th Congress, 1360.

[2] *Ibid.*, 1381–2.   [3] *Ibid.*, 1360.

ures of the original bill; it substituted "President" for
"General," in the second section, and, in place of the provision against writs of *habeas corpus*, the fourth section
simply enacted that "all persons put under military arrest
by virtue of this act shall be tried without unnecessary delay,
and no cruel or unusual punishment shall be inflicted."
The fifth section contained the features proposed in the
Bingham and Blaine amendments, amplified in a manner
satisfactory to the majority of the Senatorial caucus. The
conditions of readmission were as follows: The adoption
of a constitution in conformity with the Constitution of
the United States, and the ratification of the 14th amendment. The constitution, which must be examined and
approved by Congress, must be framed by a convention of
delegates chosen by "the male citizens of said State twenty-
one years of age and upwards, of whatever race, color, or
previous condition, who have been resident in the State for
one year previous to the day of such election, except such
as may be disfranchised for participation in the rebellion, or
for felony at common law;" must give the elective franchise to all qualified as electors for the delegates; and must
be ratified by a majority of the persons voting on ratification, and qualified as such electors. To this the proviso was
added that no person disqualified by the 14th amendment
from holding office should be chosen as a delegate to the
convention or vote for members of it. One more amendment to the bill was made on motion of Senator Doolittle.
This added as a proviso to the fourth section: "That no
sentence of death under the provisions of this act shall be
carried into effect without the approval of the President."

The bill was returned to the House in this form, the Senate
having passed it at six o'clock Sunday morning, February
17. The margin of time that could be used without permitting the bill to be killed by a "pocket veto" was now very

limited, but the House refused to concur in the amendment and called for a committee of conference, February 19. The Senate insisted on its amendment and the bill was again returned to the House, which on the following day concurred in the Senate amendment, but added an amendment of its own proposed by Mr. Wilson, of Iowa, and amended on motion of Mr. Shellabarger.[1] This amendment, constituting the sixth section of the bill, was speedily concurred in by the Senate, and on February 20, 1867, the bill was finally passed and ready for the President's veto.

The sixth section, so hurriedly tacked on to the bill, was of no slight importance, as it declared in legal form the *status* of the Southern governments, and clinched the qualifications for the elective franchise. It provided that "until the people of said rebel States shall be by law admitted to representation in the Congress of the United States, any civil governments which may exist therein shall be deemed provisional only, and in all respects subject to the paramount authority of the United States at any time to abolish, modify, control, or supersede the same; and in all elections to any office under such provisional governments all persons shall be entitled to vote, and none others, who are entitled to vote under the provisions of the fifth section of this act; and no person shall be eligible to any office under any such provisional governments who would be disqualified from holding office under the provisions of the third article of said constitutional amendment."[2]

As had been expected, Johnson withheld his veto as long as it was possible for him to do so without permitting the bill to become a law, not returning the bill until March 2.[3] This was done in the hope that the minority, by dilatory

---

[1] *Congressional Globe*, 2d Session, 39th Congress, 1399.

[2] McPherson, *History of the Reconstruction*, 192.

[3] *House Journal*, 2d Session, 39th Congress, 563–572.

proceedings, might prevent action on the veto before the adjournment, on March 4, and so prevent the bill from becoming a law. But the plan failed, and the bill was immediately passed, "the objections of the President to the contrary notwithstanding."

The veto message embodied an exhaustive review of the bill, a criticism of its "cruelty," and an attack upon its constitutionality. It denied the statement in the preamble that "no legal State governments or adequate protection for life or property," existed in these ten States, and declared that "the establishment of peace and good order is not its real object. * * * The military rule which it establishes is plainly to be used, not for any purpose of order or for the prevention of crime, but solely as a means of coercing the people into the adoption of principles and measures to which it is known that they are opposed, and upon which they have an undeniable right to exercise their own judgment." The despotic authority given to the commander of a district was vigorously denounced, and all the humane provisions of the bill were declared to depend upon the will of the commander, who could nullify them and oppress the people without limitations of any kind. "It reduces the whole population of the ten States—all persons, of every color, sex and condition, and every stranger within their limits—to the most abject and degrading slavery."

But aside from its injustice, Johnson went on to argue, the measure was unconstitutional and could not legally be carried into execution. In a time of peace martial law could not be established, in proof of which statement he quoted from the decision of the Supreme Court, in *Ex parte* Milligan, defining military jurisdiction. The denial of the right of trial by jury and of the privilege of the writ of *habeas corpus* was not counterbalanced by the poor privilege of trial "without unnecessary delay." In defiance of the constitutional prohibition of bills of attainder, "here is a bill of attainder against nine millions of people at once"—a legislative enactment "based upon an accusation so vague as to be scarcely intelligible, and found to be true upon no credible evidence." The primary purpose of the bill, to compel these States "by force to the adoption of organic laws and regulations which they are unwilling to accept if left to themselves," was in itself unconstitutional. "The Federal Government has no jurisdiction, authority, or power to regulate such subjects for any State."

Respecting the legality of the state governments, the important point was made that if they were illegal, their ratification of the 13th amendment could not have been legal. The message closed with an appeal for restoration "by simple compliance with the plain requirements of the Constitution."

Taken as a whole, the message unquestionably contained many strong arguments against the bill, and was virtually a summary of the arguments advanced by the minority in Congress. But the struggle had passed beyond the province of unbiased debate, and each side was equally determined not to yield any point. A measure open to the most serious suspicions regarding its constitutionality, was passed by an inflexible majority, settled in the belief that the condition of the South required the measure, and that the Constitution must accordingly be stretched to cover the case.

Those supporters of the bill who were recognized as the most careful in their judgments confidently asserted that that portion of it establishing the military districts contained nothing that could not have been carried out legally by the government as a military measure, without the formality of enacting the bill. The insurrectionary States would legally remain in a condition of insurrection until Congress should formally declare the insurrection to be at end. Consequently martial law could constitutionally prevail, trial by jury and the writ of *habeas corpus* be suspended, and civil government utilized as an aid to military rule, to any extent that might seem advisable to the general in charge. The claim that the measure amounted to an enormous bill of attainder was immediately dismissed as absurd, as no corruption of blood or forfeiture of estates was involved, and the whole measure was avowedly temporary, to cease as soon as the State should comply with the conditions of reconstruction.

Congress felt justified in passing the bill over the veto, and accordingly the general process of reconstruction was established with conditions far more onerous than had been intended in the first session of the 39th Congress. The provisions of the act immediately went into force, and the commanders of the districts were appointed on March eleventh.

3. The bill was conceded by all its supporters to be incomplete. It provided for the establishment of districts and the governing of these districts by military law, and it was hoped that the immediate crying need of a strong government to enforce order and prevent the continuance of the oppression of the freedmen was satisfied. This done, they could proceed more deliberately to the enactment of measures which would provide the mechanism for carrying out the provisions of the fifth section. The adjournment of the 39th Congress at noon of March 4 prevented any action until the next Congress; but preparation had been made for such an emergency by an act which provided that in future each Congress should convene upon the adjournment of its predecessor.[1]

The 40th Congress at once settled down to work upon the problem. Chief Justice Chase prepared a bill which was used as a basis for the discussion. Senator Wilson and

---

[1] Act of January 22, 1867.

others modified the bill to some extent, and introduced it in the Senate on March 7.[1] The same bill, slightly modified, was introduced in the House.[2] Considerable trouble was experienced in agreeing upon the details of the bill, but on March 19 both houses finally adopted a compromise proposed by a committee of conference. The veto message of the President was received four days later; the bill was immediately passed over the veto and became a law.[3]

As finally passed, the bill was entitled: "An Act supplementary to an Act entitled, 'An Act to provide for the more efficient government of the rebel States,' passed March second, eighteen hundred and sixty-seven, and to facilitate restoration." It enacted that the commanding general in each district should cause a registration to be made before September 1, 1867, of those entitled to vote under the original act, and should require all registering to take the following oath: "I, ———, do solemnly swear (or affirm) in the presence of Almighty God, that I am a citizen of the State of ———; that I have resided in said State for —— months next preceding this day, and now reside in the county of ———, or the parish of ———, in said State (as the case may be); that I am twenty-one years old; that I have not been disfranchised for participation in any rebellion or civil war against the United States, nor for felony committed against the laws of any State or of the United States; that I have never been a member of any State legislature, nor held any executive or judicial office in any State and afterwards engaged in insurrection or rebellion against the United States, or given aid or comfort

---

[1] *Congressional Globe*, 1st Session, 40th Congress, 13.

[2] The Committee on the Judiciary was instructed on March 7 to report a supplementary bill (*Congressional Globe*, 17), and the Wilson bill was accordingly reported by it.

[3] *Congressional Globe*, 1st Session, 40th Congress, 302–3; 313–14.

to the enemies thereof; that I have never taken an oath as a member of Congress of the United States, or as an officer of the United States, or as a member of any State legislature, or as an executive or judicial officer of any State, to support the Constitution of the United States, and afterwards engaged in insurrection or rebellion against the United States or given aid or comfort to the enemies thereof; that I will faithfully support the Constitution and obey the laws of the United States, and will, to the best of my ability, encourage others so to do, so help me God." [1] After the completion of the registration in any State, it was provided that there should be held, after at least thirty days' public notice by the commanding general, an election of delegates "to a convention for the purpose of establishing a constitution and civil government for such State loyal to the Union." This convention was to consist of the same number of members as the most numerous branch of the State legislature in 1860. [2] Those voting at the election of delegates were also to vote for or against the holding of the convention, and it was not to be held if a majority of the ballots was cast against it, or if a majority of the registered voters failed to vote on the question. Boards were to be appointed by the commanding general to superintend the registration and election, and make returns to him of the results of the election. The convention was required to assemble at a place and time appointed by the commanding general, by a notice to be given by him within sixty days from the date of election; and to frame a constitution according to the provisions of the original and the present act. The constitution so framed was then to be submitted to the registered voters at

---

[1] *Congressional Globe*, appendix, 1st Session, 40th Congress, 39; McPherson, *History of the Reconstruction*, 192.

[2] Except in Virginia, where the number was modified in proportion to the change made by the separation of West Virginia.

an election conducted by officials who were to be appointed by the commanding general, and who were to make returns to him. In case the constitution was ratified " by a majority of the votes of the registered electors qualified as herein specified, cast at said election (at least one-half of all the registered voters voting upon the question of such ratification)," it was provided that the president of the convention should "transmit a copy of the same, duly certified, to the President of the United States, who shall forthwith transmit the same to Congress," and that, if Congress should be satisfied that all the provisions of the acts were carried out, and that no force or fraud was used, and should approve the constitution, the State should " be declared entitled to representation, and senators and representatives shall be admitted therefrom as therein provided." It was further provided that all elections in the States mentioned in the original act should, during the operation of that act, be by ballot; that the officials in charge of the registration and elections must take the " iron-clad " oath of July 2, 1862;[1] that the expenses incurred by the commanding generals in carrying out the act should be paid out of the treasury, but

---

[1] By the act of that date all persons elected or appointed to any office under the government of the United States were required to take the following oath previous to entering upon the duties of such office: " I, A. B., do solemnly swear (or affirm) that I have never voluntarily borne arms against the United States since I have been a citizen thereof; that I have voluntarily given no aid, countenance, counsel, or encouragement to persons engaged in armed hostility thereto; that I have neither sought nor accepted nor attempted to exercise the functions of any office whatever, under any authority or pretended authority in hostility to the United States; that I have not yielded a voluntary support to any pretended government, authority, power or constitution within the United States, hostile or inimical thereto. And I do further swear (or affirm) that, to the best of my knowledge and ability, I will support and defend the Constitution of the United States against all enemies, foreign and domestic; that I will bear true faith and allegiance to the same; that I take this obligation freely, without any mental reservation or purpose of evasion, and that I will well and faithfully discharge the duties of the office on which I am about to enter, so help me God."

that the state conventions should provide for the levying of taxes to pay other expenses.[1]

The veto message on this bill was much shorter than that on the original reconstruction measure. The President said: "No consideration could induce me to give my approval to such an election law for any purpose, and especially for the great purpose of framing the constitution of a State. If ever the American citizen should be left to the free exercise of his own judgment, it is when he is engaged in the work of forming the fundamental law under which he is to live." He animadverted upon the extreme looseness of the provisions in regard to the registration boards, and upon the great powers vested in them. The main objections to the bill were of course those which he had stated in the veto of March 2.

The passage of the supplementary reconstruction act, and of a joint resolution providing for the expenses involved in carrying out the provisions of the act, completed the work of this session of the 40th Congress. It was hoped that no further congressional action would be needed until the constitutions of the States should be submitted for examination and approval, preparatory to granting representation. But the importance of the measures and the avowed hostility of the President caused hesitation on the part of Congress as to adjourning till the regular December session. It was realized that if any loop-hole could be found by which the intention of the act could be evaded, Johnson would have no hesitation in taking advantage of it. To provide for such a contingency Congress passed a concurrent resolution which provided for a recess until July 3, and authorized the President of the Senate and the Speaker of the House to adjourn Congress until the first Monday in December if a quorum did not appear on July 3. In case

[1] Appendix, *Congressional Globe*, 1st Session, 40th Congress, 39, 40.

everything appeared to be progressing with little friction, the members would not assemble; but if there should be any unfavorable developments, Congress could assemble independently of the President and enact legislation to remedy the difficulty.

4. July 3 found a quorum in both houses. The Attorney-General had rendered an opinion upon the act of March 2 which greatly hampered the work of the commanders of the districts. He advised the President that the act should be construed strictly, that the commanders should be allowed no powers beyond those specifically bestowed upon them. This prevented them from removing state officers, from making new laws for the government of the people, or from suspending the action of the state courts; and with state officers hostile to the federal authorities, and using every means to impede their work, the commanders found it impossible properly to discharge the duties assigned to them by the act.[1] The intent of the reconstruction acts obviously was to make the commanders of the districts commanders *de facto* as well as *de jure*. Consequently remedial legislation was deemed necessary, and Congress convened for the purpose of framing additional acts defining more precisely the intention of the preceding acts and the powers of the commanders.

A few days' debate sufficed to bring Congress to an agreement as to the form of a second supplementary act. The bill passed both Houses on July 13, was vetoed on the 19th, and was immediately passed over the veto.[2] It declared[3] the true intent and meaning of the previous reconstruction acts to be that the governments then existing in the ten States specified in the acts were illegal, and that such governments, "if

[1] Johnson, *Reconstruction*, in Lalor, iii, 552; Cox, *Three Decades of Federal Legislation*, 378.

[2] *Congressional Globe*, appendix, 1st Session, 39th Congress, 43–4.

[3] McPherson, *History of the Reconstruction*, 335–6.

continued, were to be continued subject in all respects to the military commanders of the respective districts, and to the paramount authority of Congress." It therefore provided that the district commanders should have the power to suspend or remove all incumbents of offices of "any so-called State or the government thereof," and to fill all vacancies in such offices, however caused. The same powers were granted to the General of the Army, who was also empowered to disapprove the appointments or removals made by the district commanders. The previous appointments by the district commanders were confirmed and made subject to the provisions of the act, and it was declared to be the duty of these commanders to remove from office all who were disloyal to the United States, or who opposed in any way the administration of the reconstruction acts. The registration boards were empowered and required "before allowing the registration of any person to ascertain, upon such facts or information as they can obtain, whether such person is entitled to be registered."[1] No person was to be disqualified as a member of any board of registration by reason of race or color. The true intent and meaning of the oath prescribed in the supplementary act was fully explained, the most important portion of the explanation being that the words "executive or judicial office in any State" should be construed to "include all civil offices created by law for the administration of any general law of a State, or for the administration of justice." The time of registration under the supplementary act was extended to October 1, 1867, in the discretion of the commander; and it was provided that

---

[1] Stanbery had ruled that the willingness of an applicant to take the oath must be regarded as final evidence of his qualification to register. Thus those notoriously incapacitated from taking the oath honestly, could not be prevented from registering. This additional power virtually enabled the boards of registration to exercise their own discretion as to whom they should enroll.

"the boards of registration shall have power, and it shall be their duty, commencing fourteen days prior to any election under said act, and upon reasonable notice of the time and place thereof, to revise, for a period of five days, the registration lists," by striking out the names of those found to be disqualified, and adding the names of those qualified for registration. Executive pardon or amnesty should not qualify any one for registration who without it would be disqualified. District commanders were empowered "to remove any member of a board of registration, and to appoint another in his stead, and to fill any vacancy in such board." The iron-clad oath was to be required of all registration boards, and of all persons elected or appointed to office in the military districts. Further possibility of unfavorable construction by the Attorney-General was prevented by the provision that "no district commander or member of the board of registration, or any of the officers or appointees acting under them, shall be bound in his action by any opinion of any civil officer of the United States." The closing section, taken in connection with this, was fully as significant: "All the provisions of this act and of the acts to which this is supplementary shall be construed liberally, to the end that all the intents thereof may be fully and perfectly carried out."

5. Reconstruction under the provisions of these three acts was rapidly accomplished in most of the States.[1] In some of the districts the commanders probably were too severe upon the whites, but in the main the intent of the acts was carried out with as little harshness as could well be expected. Those qualified were registered, conventions were held, and constitutions were framed and submitted to the people for their ratification according to the provisions of the acts. Alabama was the first State to vote upon a new consti-

[1] Scott, *Reconstruction during the Civil War*, 317 ff.

tution, and the Democrats, or Conservatives, as they styled themselves, took advantage of the fifth section of the act of March 23, which required at least one-half of the registered voters to vote on the question of ratification, as a condition of the validity of the election. Non-action seemed to be the easiest method of defeating the constitution, and they accordingly absented themselves from the polls, only 70,812, out of 165,812 registered voters, casting their ballots.[1]

6. There had been a strong minority in Congress opposed to the insertion of this section, who had foreseen this very outcome; and the action of Alabama converted the minority into a majority. A third supplementary bill was accordingly passed. Johnson neither signed nor vetoed it; and it became a law without his signature on March 11, 1868. It provided that in future all elections authorized by the act of March 23, 1867, "should be decided by a majority of the votes actually cast," thus preventing any repetition of the Alabama experiment.[2]

7. The constitution submitted in Mississippi was rejected. Constitutions were not submitted in Texas and Virginia until a later date. The other States ratified their constitutions by large majorities, and on June 22 the act " to admit the State of Arkansas to representation in Congress " became a law.

8. Three days later the act admitting North Carolina, South Carolina, Louisiana, Georgia, Alabama and Florida to representation, became a law. Both bills were passed over the President's vetoes, Johnson to the last refusing to recognize even in the most indirect way the constitutionality of the congressional plan.

Eight of the eleven States were now nominally reconstructed, but in fact they were only entering upon that most trying period of their history—the era of "carpet-bag

[1] Cox, *Three Decades of Federal Legislation*, 512–14.

[2] McPherson, *History of the Reconstruction*, 336–7.

government." The whole period of reconstruction is marked by blindness and prejudice on both sides. The spirit of compromise could find no place in either's plans. "What might have been" is always a fruitless subject of discussion; but any student of the three tumultuous years following the war cannot but see that the attitude of both the North and the South prevented the adoption of the plan of reconstruction which would with the least trouble and delay, have remoulded the unwieldy mass of liberated blacks into an orderly, progressive class of citizens. At the same time he can see that the divergence of views was inevitable and that it is impossible to say to one side "You were right," and to the other "You were wrong."

CHAPTER VI.

THE IMPEACHMENT OF THE PRESIDENT.

1. In the preceding chapters we have traced step by step the development of the theory of reconstruction and the formulation of the reconstruction acts of the 39th and 40th Congresses. We have noticed the wide divergence between the ideas of Johnson and those of the Republican party, and have seen that the whole program was carried over the vetoes of the President by the overwhelming Republican majority. But the contest between the President and Congress, which had been embittered by so many personalities on both sides, did not come to an end with the passage of legislation which fully embodied the congressional theory, but continued until it culminated in a desperate effort of the Republican party to remove Johnson from the presidential chair.

The very conditions under which he assumed the presidential office rendered his position difficult, and made estrangement of the executive and legislative departments an easy matter. On the particular issue of reconstruction Lincoln and Congress were at variance; but the tragic nature of Lincoln's death caused this matter to be forgotten in the overwhelming sense of the loss of the man who had safely guided the government through the most trying years of its history. But, for a Congress so extremely Northern and Republican, with antagonisms and prejudices which only fratricidal wars can create, to be compelled to work with a man not only a Southerner, but practically a Democrat, must of necessity bring about a crisis.

Moreover, the flourishing condition of the spoils system served to aggravate the antagonism between the two departments. History shows that, while selfish motives are always indignantly repudiated by politicians, they account for many of the more important political movements of the century. With the immense federal patronage at his disposal, Johnson realized that he had a powerful instrument of revenge at hand, and he did not hesitate to use it. At a time when every congressman was under the strongest pressure from his home constituency, inability to gratify the demands of the voracious office-seeker was indeed a cause for bitterness.

We can thus easily distinguish three causes which, working together upon a strongly Republican Congress, resulted in the attempted removal of the President. First, the antagonism arising from different fundamental political ideas, the strained conditions of the times, and the woeful tactlessness of Johnson; second, the almost morbid yet natural fears of the Republican party regarding the sometime seceded States; third, the anger aroused by the use of federal patronage to further the interests of the President.

2. Impeachment, however, was too serious a matter for Congress to enter upon lightly. Art. II, sec. iv, of the Constitution provides for impeachment as follows: "The President, Vice-President and all civil officers of the United States shall be removed from office on impeachment for, and conviction of, treason, bribery, or other high crimes and misdemeanors." Obviously the President had not committed and would not commit anything that could legally be called treason or bribery: Had he done or would he do anything which could be construed as a high crime or misdemeanor? The answer largely depended upon the person's point of view. The extreme radical held that Johnson's whole career as President could be considered as an attempt treasonably to reinstate the Southern States in a position of power. The

more moderate Republicans could not be made to acquiesce in this view, and it soon became evident that Johnson would never be brought to trial on impeachment, unless he could be made to violate some clearly defined law. The radical element, however, did not easily accept this situation. By every means possible they tried to force the moderates into line. The whole past career of the President was critically studied, and every act which could by any possible means be construed as a breach of presidential duty was put in the list of offences for which he should be tried. But all to no purpose. Something more tangible must be produced, or the trial would never occur.

3. Notwithstanding the evident indisposition on the part of many to proceed to extreme measures, the radicals determined to force matters to an issue, if possible. Under Mr. James M. Ashley of Ohio as leader, the attack was begun shortly after the opening of the second session of the Thirty-ninth Congress. On December 17, 1866, Mr. Ashley moved to suspend the rules so as to permit him to report a resolution from the Committee on Territories. His motion was not agreed to, and the first step towards impeachment was therefore a failure. The motion is of interest, however, as evidencing the deliberate intention of the radicals to discover some act which would justify impeachment. The resolution provided for a select committee who were to inquire " whether any acts have been done by any officer of the Government of the United States which in contemplation of the Constitution are high crimes or misdemeanors, and whether said acts were designed or calculated to overthrow, subvert or corrupt the Government of the United States, or any department thereof."

Again on January 7 resolutions looking to impeachment were offered by Mr. Ashley and two other persons. Mr. Ashley's resolution was adopted, while the others were re-

ferred to the Committee on Reconstruction and the Committee on the Judiciary.   The resolutions which were referred
gave as a reason for impeachment, " the purpose of securing
the fruits of the victories gained on the part of the republic
during the late war, waged by rebels and traitors against the
life of the nation "—a decidedly strong statement to make,
in view of the predominance of the Republican party at the
time, and its ability to render nugatory any attempt of the
President to take away from the republic " the fruits of the
victories gained."   Exaggerated expressions of this sort
show how far the contest had degenerated from a conflict of
opinions as to the constitutional position of the revolted
States, into a personal warfare.   Another significant reason
for impeachment given in these resolutions was, that it
was necessary in order to give " effect to the will of the
people as expressed at the polls during the recent elections
by a majority numbering in the aggregate more than four
hundred thousand votes."   It has already been shown how
disastrously the campaign resulted for Johnson, and how it
furnished popular sanction for the radical reconstruction
legislation which was passed over the presidential vetoes.
But, to assume that a popular expression of disapproval of
the President's political program made impeachment a moral
necessity, was to assume a novel position.   It was also declared in these resolutions that the President was to be
impeached for the high crimes and misdemeanors " of which
he is manifestly and notoriously guilty, and which render it
unsafe longer to permit him to exercise the powers he has
unlawfully assumed."

These expressions seeming to be too indefinite, the specific
charges submitted by Mr. Ashley met with more favor, and
were accordingly adopted.   These charges centered about
an alleged " usurpation of power and violation of law" which
was to be found in corrupt uses of the appointing, pardoning,

and veto powers, improper disposition of public offices and
corrupt interference in elections. These were clinched again
by the general charge that the President had "committed
acts which, in contemplation of the Constitution, are high
crimes and misdemeanors,"—a charge obviously introduced
to include any points which might in the future be made
against him.

4. As the event proved, the attempt to bring matters to a
successful issue in the 39th Congress was a failure. The
Committee on the Judiciary went to work vigorously, calling
many witnesses and collecting as much material as possible;
but on the 28th of February it reported, with only one dissenting voice, that in spite of all its efforts not enough testimony had been gathered to warrant any report beyond a
recommendation that the investigation be continued. The
ninth member of the committee, Mr. Rogers of New Jersey,
reported emphatically that a careful examination of the
subject had convinced him that "there is not a particle of
evidence to sustain any of the charges," and that "the case
is wholly without a particle of evidence upon which an impeachment could be founded." He further declared that
but little of the testimony taken would be admitted in the
courts, and that the whole matter should be dropped, as it
would certainly end "in a complete vindication of the President." Logically, the standpoint of Mr. Rogers was a correct one. From a strictly legal view of the case, there was
very serious doubt as to the advisability of attempting impeachment; but the opponents of the President counted
upon their large majority to force the matter, and the line
of action recommended by the majority of the committee
was adopted.

As has been seen, the 40th Congress assembled immediately upon the adjournment of the 39th; and on March
7, 1867, the new Judiciary Committee was authorized to

proceed with the investigation, and to continue it during any recess the House might take. By another resolution agreed to March 29, the committee was requested to report immediately upon the reassembling of Congress, which was to be in the following July, if political conditions seemed to require it.[1]

The committee accordingly continued its investigations, but, though the radicals felt sure that it was composed of men who would favor impeachment, it at first reported by a majority of five to four against impeachment. A recommitment resulted in the conversion of one member of the committee[2] to impeachment views; and on November 25 Mr. Boutwell, of Massachusetts, reported from the committee a resolution impeaching the President for high crimes and misdemeanors.

5. The debate on this resolution was entered upon in December, 1867, and was marked by the effort on the part of the radicals to support a most indefinite and general charge. In spite of the thoroughness of the investigation of the Judiciary Committee, in which neither time nor expense had been spared, the attitude of the moderates was justified. Nothing had been unearthed which from the legal standpoint could be considered a high crime or misdemeanor. Failing in this, Mr. Boutwell assumed the ground that the evidence showed that President Johnson had been deliberately using his office to bring back, so far as possible, the Democratic party into power, and that his efforts to restore the insurrectionary States to their former power had been in the interest of the rebellion.

Although most Republicans at this time could not believe that the inhabitants of the Southern States were sincere in

[1] McPherson, 190.

[2] Dunning, in *Papers of the American Historical Association*, iv, 473; *Congressional Globe*, 1st Session, 40th Congress, p. 565.

their protestations of a desire to lay aside all differences and once more become loyal citizens, there were many who could not agree to Mr. Boutwell's definition of high crimes and misdemeanors; and these moderate Republicans, aided by the Democrats, defeated the resolution by a vote of one hundred and eight to fifty-seven.[1] The attempt to impeach without definite legal charges had failed.

But the President soon gave the House the very opportunity it desired. While the direct attack upon the President was being carried on by means of the effort to impeach him, an indirect attack was made by the legislative limitation of his powers. One of the cries of alarmists had been that there was danger that the President might in some way take advantage of his constitutional position as commander-in-chief of the army and navy, so as to injure the government and advance his own interests. Some went even farther and declared that he designed with the aid of the army to overthrow the government, and place the United States in the power of the rebels. Such charges, viewed from the standpoint of history, seem too absurd for consideration, but during the reconstruction period the feverish condition of the country made possible the acceptance of almost any startling rumor.

6. But even those who did not apprehend that Johnson would use the army for any improper purpose, were willing to limit his power and prestige by depriving him of his military authority; and this was accordingly done by a section introduced into the army appropriation bill.[2] This section required all orders to the army to be made through the General of the Army, thus practically making his approval of them necessary. It also prevented the President or the Secretary of War from removing, suspending or relieving from command the General of the Army, and even forbade

[1] McPherson. 264,   [2] *Ibid.*, 178.

his being assigned for duty away from headquarters, except at his own request. This had the effect of taking away from the President all his constitutional powers as commander-in-chief. As the section was put as a rider on an appropriation bill and a veto must cover the whole bill, Johnson contented himself with a simple protest and returned the act with his signature.[1]

7. The attack upon the civil powers of the President was made through the Tenure-of-Office Act.[2] As the violation of this act was the ground of the most serious charge in the impeachment trial, a somewhat detailed study of its provisions, and of the views expressed by the President in his veto of it, is advisable. The bill provided that " every person holding any civil office to which he has been appointed by and with the advice and consent of the Senate," and every person so appointed in the future, should be entitled to hold such office until a successor should have been appointed in like manner, that is to say, *with the advice and consent of the Senate*. The only liberty of action allowed the President was during the recess of the Senate, when he was permitted to suspend an officer until the next meeting of the Senate, and appoint a *pro tempore* official. Within twenty days after the meeting of the Senate, however, he was required to give his reasons for the suspension. If the Senate approved of the removal, a permanent appointment was to be made ; if they refused to concur, the suspended officer was immediately to resume his duties. Any violation of this act by the President was made an impeachable offense, by the declaration that " every removal, appointment, or employment made, had, or exercised, contrary to the provisions of this act * * * are hereby declared to be high misdemeanors."

[1] McPherson, 178.

[2] Vetoed March 2, 1867, and repassed by both houses on the same day. For copy of the act, see McPherson, 176 ff.

The other provisions were of minor importance, and do not require notice here.

The veto message of the President was a calm, dignified and judicial discussion of the constitutionality of the bill, and was in every way a creditable document, sustaining fully the high character of his previous vetoes. He called attention to the fact that the whole question of the authority of the President in cases of removal from office had been discussed thoroughly in Congress as early as 1789, and decided in favor of the President. He quoted Madison's argument to prove that all executive power, except what is specifically excepted, is vested in the President, and that as no exception was made as to the power of removal, it must be vested in him. He also cited many possible cases, in which it would be absolutely necessary for the President to possess the power of removal.[1] A decision of the Supreme Court was referred to,[2] in which it was observed that both the legislative and the executive department had assumed in practice that the power of removal was vested in the President alone. When, for instance, the Departments of State, War and the Treasury were created in 1789, provision was made for a subordinate who should take charge of the office " when the head of the Department should be removed *by the President of the United States.*" Story, Kent and Webster were all quoted as affirming the same legislative construction of the Constitution. The great practical value of the power during the Civil War was noticed, and its present and future necessity strongly urged; and the message closed with an earnest appeal to Congress not to violate the original spirit of the Constitution.

8. The passage of the bill over the veto placed Johnson

[1] His argument here, however, is weak, as the power of suspension would easily have covered all such cases.

[2] *Ex parte* Hennen, January, 1839, 13 Peters, 139.

in a situation in which a collision was almost sure to come. As the chief executive of the country he was charged with the duty of carrying out the provisions of the reconstruction acts, notwithstanding his strong personal repugnance to them. Under the advice of Attorney-General Stanbery he had construed the acts literally, and he had thus frustrated in part the object of the legislation. But the co-operation of the army was necessary, and unfortunately for President Johnson, the Secretary of War, Mr. Stanton, strongly opposed his views, and conducted himself as far as possible in accordance with the wishes of the congressional majority. The continued friction between the President and the Secretary of War seemed to President Johnson to necessitate Stanton's retirement, but repeated hints to that effect were not recognized by the latter. Finally, on August 5, 1867, the President informed him that "public considerations of a high character constrained" him to say that his resignation would be accepted. The Secretary's prompt reply was that "public considerations of a high character" constrained him not to resign until the next session of Congress. A week later, August 12, the President formally suspended him and appointed General Grant Secretary *ad interim.*[1] Stanton then submitted "under protest to superior force."

When Congress met in December the President reported his suspension of Stanton, and after long discussion the Senate, on January 13, 1868, refused to concur.[2] When informed of this action of the Senate, General Grant immediately turned over the Secretary's office to Stanton, thus definitely committing himself to the congressional interpretation of the law. Grant's action was a sore disappointment to the President. Johnson had refused to accept the Tenure-of-Office Act as constitutional, and had purposed to make this a test case. In the correspondence which passed be-

[1] McPherson, 261.   [2] *Ibid.*, 262.

tween him and General Grant after the latter's acquiescence
in the action of the Senate, Johnson claimed that it was
understood that Grant was either to refuse to give up the
office to Stanton, or, if he should be unwilling to take so
prominent a part in the contest, to resign and permit the
office to be filled with some one whose views agreed with the
President's, so that Stanton, if he sought to regain the office,
might be compelled to resort to the courts.   In this way the
constitutionality of the act could be tested.   Johnson's statements as to the understanding with Grant were substantially
endorsed by the Cabinet, on the strength of a conversation
between Johnson and Grant at a cabinet meeting.   Grant,
however, firmly denied that there was any such agreement
or understanding.[1]

A few days after Stanton had resumed his duties as Secretary of War, the President sought to put in operation a plan
for rendering his possession of the office ineffective.   On
January 19, he ordered General Grant, in charge of the
army, to disregard all of Stanton's orders unless he knew
directly from the President that they were the latter's orders.[2]
The order was repeated in writing at Grant's request on January 29.   On the following day, Grant refused to carry it out,
declaring that an order from Secretary Stanton would be considered satisfactory evidence that it was authorized by the Executive.[3]   This correspondence between Johnson and Grant
was subsequently called for by Congress, and an attempt was
made to frame articles of impeachment on the ground that
the President was instructing Grant to disobey the orders
of his superior.   Careful examination of the legal bearings
of the question convinced a majority of the Reconstruction
Committee that nothing would be gained by inserting charges

[1] The text of the correspondence between Grant and Johnson may be found in
McPherson, *History of the Reconstruction*, p. 282 ff.

[2] McPherson, p. 283.   [3] *Ibid.*, p. 284.

based on this correspondence. The President had shrewdly
worded his communication so as not to violate any legal
technicalities.[1]

Having failed in his first two attacks upon Stanton, Johnson finally resorted to a still stronger measure. Completely
ignoring the Tenure-of-Office Act, he addressed a letter to
Stanton, February 21, removing him from office, and direct-
ing him to transfer all the property of the War Department to
Adjutant General Lorenzo Thomas. Thomas, having received his appointment as secretary *ad interim*, proceeded
to the office and formally demanded possession. Stanton
avoided giving a direct answer to the demand, and on
the following morning Gen. Thomas was arrested for
violation of the Tenure-of-Office Act. After bail had been
procured he renewed his demand, but Stanton ignored his
appointment. Several plans were devised by the President
and Thomas' lawyers to make the contest center around
Thomas, but the congressional managers decided to drop
the matter, and concentrate their energies upon a presidential impeachment.[2]

The last step of the President opened the way for immediate action. Violation of the Tenure-of-Office Act was
explicitly declared an impeachable offense, and as to the flagrancy of its violation by the order of February 21 there could
be no question. Many of the wavering Republicans now had
their doubts of the expediency of impeachment cleared away,
and on February 24 the resolution formally impeaching the
President of "high crimes and misdemeanors in office" was
passed.[3]

9. On March 2, the first nine articles of impeachment

[1] McPherson, 265. The fact also that Grant had refused to be governed by
Johnson's instructions made the attempt still less serious.

[2] See Dunning, *Papers American Historical Association*, 1890, p. 481.

[3] McPherson, 266. The vote was 128 to 47, divided strictly on party lines.

were adopted; two additional articles were added on the 3d; and on the 4th they were presented to the Senate. On March 30, the trial began. The articles charged the President with high crimes and misdemeanors in respect of the order for the removal of Stanton, the appointment of Thomas as Secretary of War *ad interim*, the attempt to hinder Stanton in the exercise of his lawful duties, the wilful violation of the Tenure-of-Office Act, the attempt to seize the properties of the War Department, the attempt unlawfully to disburse moneys through the appointment of Thomas, an attempt to make General Emory violate the Tenure-of-Office Act, the attempt to injure the good reputation of the legislative department by speeches delivered at various specified places, and his determined opposition to the reconstruction policy as outlined in the various acts of Congress.[1]

These articles were very sweeping, and were designed as a sort of drag-net to include all of the complaints which could possibly be brought against the President. Yet the House of Representatives, previous to the attempted removal of Secretary Stanton, after the most searching examination into the President's record, had failed to find sufficient ground on which to base an impeachment. Therefore the only charges that deserved really serious attention were those growing out of the violation of the Tenure-of-Office Act. In the President's reply to the charges he explains his attitude on this matter. In his opinion the Tenure-of-Office Act was unconstitutional. The very fact that he as Executive was legally held responsible for the acts of the Secretary of War made it necessary for him to exercise the power of removal or of indefinite suspension. He had at first complied with the letter of the act in order to avoid a further struggle with Congress; but, hav-

---

[1] For the full text of the eleven articles, see McPherson, 266 ff. For a critical discussion of the legal points involved in the trial, see Dunning, in *Papers American Historical Association*, iv, 483 ff.

ing been frustrated by Congress in his design, the only alternative that remained to him, in view of his strained relations
with the Secretary of War, was the latter's unconditional removal.

10. The President's case, as to the constitutionality of his
action and the unconstitutionality of the Tenure-of-Office
Act, was strong, and was presented with great ability by the
President's counsel. But, from the very beginning, it was
obvious that the case would be determined mainly on
political lines.

If the Republican party could hold all the Republican
Senators to the decision of the majority, a verdict of guilty
was assured. Consequently, the strongest efforts were made
to bring all into line. But some proved recalcitrant. The
prospect that the President of the United States was to be
forced out of his office as a punishment for his opposition to
the Legislative Department was not edifying. Hitherto the
presidential office had possessed great dignity. To be sure,
Johnson's conduct had gone far towards the destruction of
that dignity, but a conviction on impeachment charges would
drag down the office immeasurably. Some of the Senators
also realized that the tendency of Congress during the whole
struggle had been towards an encroachment upon the executive powers, and that there was serious danger that the balance of the governmental system might be destroyed. While,
therefore, they strongly disapproved of Johnson's conduct,
they felt unwilling to expose the government to the shock
which would accompany his removal from the presidential
chair. The trial proceeded slowly and the case was ably
contested by counsel on both sides; but the prosecution
was practically brought to a close on May 16, by the vote
which was taken on the eleventh article of impeachment.
This article was chosen for the first test of strength, because
it embodied those charges which had caused the most feel-

ing, and which were best calculated to cause Senators to
cast aside judicial restraints and vote according to their prejudices. But, seven Republicans refused to line themselves
with the radical majority. They and the twelve Democratic
Senators voted for acquittal. Thirty-five Republicans voted
" guilty," but this lacked one of the needful two-thirds majority. Ten days later another vote was taken on the second
and third articles, with the same result. The fight was then
given up, and the court of impeachment was declared ad-
journed.

11. It was a fortunate thing for the country that the
attempt failed. The convulsions of the Civil War had unsettled most seriously our conceptions of the relations of the
three co-ordinate departments of the government. Lincoln
had not hesitated to assume powers totally outside the ordi-
nary functions of the Executive. The country had sustained
him in this; but, with the return of peace, and with Johnson
in the presidential chair, Congress had determined to resume
its powers. Again the country responded; but the violence
of the reaction caused the pendulum to swing too far in the
opposite direction; and our institutions were placed in
greater danger than they were in before. But, just as the
Civil War had settled the question as to the indissolubility of
the Union, so no less emphatically did the failure of the
impeachment trial confirm the equality of the three departments of our government.

AUTHORITIES.

Blaine, James G. Twenty Years of Congress. Norwich, 1884.

Congressional Globe. 37th–40th Congresses. Washington, 1861–1868.

Cooper, T. V., and Fenton, H. T. American Politics. Boston, 1890.

Cox, S. S. Three Decades of Federal Legislation. Providence, 1888.

Dunning, Wm. A. Articles on Civil War and Reconstruction, in Political Science Quarterly, vols. i. and ii., and on The Impeachment, in Papers Am. Hist. Assoc., vol. iv.

Gillet, R. H. Democracy in the United States. New York, 1868.

Herbert, Hilary A. Editor. Why the Solid South? Baltimore, 1890.

House Journal. 37th–40th Congresses. Washington, 1861–1868.

House Reports. Vol. ii., 1865–66. Washington, 1866.

House Reports. Vol. ii., 1866–67. Washington, 1867.

Hurd, J. C. Theory of our National Existence. Boston, 1881.

Johnston, Alexander. History of the United States. New York, 1891.

Johnston, Alexander. Representative American Orations. New York and London.

Johnston, Alexander. Reconstruction, Emancipation Proclamation, Freedmen's Bureau, etc., Lalor, Cyclopedia of Polit. Science. 3 vols. New York, 1890.

Lowell. J. R. Political Essays, in " Works." Vol. V. Boston and New York, 1891.

McPherson, Edward. History of the Reconstruction. Washington, 1880.

Moore, Frank. Speeches of Andrew Johnson. Boston, 1866.

Patton, J. H. The Democratic Party. New York, 1888.

Pollard, E. A. The Lost Cause Regained. New York, 1868.

Poore, Ben : Perley. Veto Messages of the Presidents of the United States. Washington, 1886.

Ridpath. History of the United States. New York and Cincinnati.

Savage, J. Life and Public Services of Andrew Johnson. New York, 1866.

Scott, E. G. Reconstruction during the Civil War. Boston and New York, 1895.

Stanwood, E. History of Presidential Elections. Boston and New York.

Senate Journal. 37th–40th Congresses. Washington, 1861–1868.

Sterne, Simon. Constitutional History and Political Development of the United States. New York and London, 1888.

Stephens, Alexander H. The War between the States. Philadelphia.

Taylor, Richard. Destruction and Reconstruction. New York, 1879.

Williams, G. W. History of the Negro Race in America. New York, 1883.

Wilson, Henry. Rise and Fall of the Slave Power in America. New York.

Wilson, Henry. History of the Reconstruction Measures. Hartford, 1868.